19.95

LC

S0-ATJ-568

2005

At ✳ Issue

Religion and Education

Tom Head, *Book Editor*

Bruce Glassman, *Vice President*
Bonnie Szumski, *Publisher*
Helen Cothran, *Managing Editor*

GREENHAVEN PRESS
An imprint of Thomson Gale, a part of The Thomson Corporation

THOMSON
━━━━━ ✳ ━━━━━ ™
GALE

Detroit • New York • San Francisco • San Diego • New Haven, Conn.
Waterville, Maine • London • Munich

© 2005 Thomson Gale, a part of The Thomson Corporation.

Thomson and Star Logo are trademarks and Gale and Greenhaven Press are registered trademarks used herein under license.

For more information, contact
Greenhaven Press
27500 Drake Rd.
Farmington Hills, MI 48331-3535
Or you can visit our Internet site at http://www.gale.com

LIBRARY OF CONGRESS CATALOGING-IN-PUBLICATION DATA

Religion and education / Tom Head, book editor.
    p. cm. — (At issue)
Includes bibliographical references and index.
ISBN 0-7377-2743-8 (lib. : alk. paper) — ISBN 0-7377-2744-6 (pbk. : alk. paper)
    1. Religion in the public schools—United States. 2. Education—Curricula—
United States. I. Head, Tom. II. At issue (San Diego, Calif.)
LC111.R39 2005
379.2'8'0873—dc22
                                                                    2004054147

Printed in the United States of America

Contents

Introduction

When James Madison proposed the Bill of Rights in 1789, it began with these words: "Congress shall make no law respecting an establishment of religion." Since that time the U.S. Supreme Court, politicians, and ordinary Americans have disagreed on exactly what these words mean. Some say that this phrase, commonly known as the Establishment Clause, only prohibits the creation of an official, government-sanctioned church. Others argue that it prohibits any infusion of religion into government institutions.

This question is especially complicated when it is applied to public schools. For more than a century after the Bill of Rights was passed, American public schools were implicitly Christian. Teachers led students in the Lord's Prayer and conveyed moral instruction from the King James Bible. These practices changed during the late nineteenth century, when an increase in Catholic immigration led to unrest over the American public schools' endorsement of Protestantism. In the early twentieth century the religious element in public schools became less pronounced. In *Engel v. Vitale* (1962) the U.S. Supreme Court eliminated it entirely by ruling that school-endorsed prayer violates the Establishment Clause. Although the debate over religion and education touches on many issues—from the teaching of evolution in science classes to use of the phrase "under God" in the Pledge of Allegiance—it is school prayer, and specifically the *Engel* case, that clearly divided Americans into two camps: those who favor religion in school, and those who do not.

The debate over religion in schools is emotionally charged not only because it focuses on philosophical beliefs, which are by definition the deepest beliefs that people hold, but also because it involves children. American children are required by law to receive an education, and most of them therefore attend public schools. Until they reach their teen years, most children are not equipped to critically analyze religious or philosophical beliefs. For this reason the public school system can have immense power over children's beliefs. Those who support religion in school argue that by removing religious influence from schools, the U.S. government implicitly endorses atheism and teaches children that religion is not relevant to everyday life. As conservative Christian activist John D. Morris argues:

> By now it should be obvious to every parent that the public school system does not exist to deepen the spiritual life of the Christian young person. While many individual teachers and the occasional local school board and administration are sympathetic, the national and state teachers' organizations and curriculum writers all have an aggressive and very liberal political agenda. . . . Christian values are not only ignored, they are taught against, and the rights of individual Christian students and teachers are denied. We wonder how Christian students can survive with a viable worldview intact.

Although Christianity is the most widely practiced religion in the United States and the only religion that has been endorsed by its public school system in the past, some religious leaders of other faiths offer similar criticisms of the strict separation of religion and education.

Meanwhile, many Americans are concerned that religion in education will reflect conservative Christianity, as it did in the nineteenth century, and exclude or unduly influence children who are not being raised in that tradition. According to Americans United for Separation of Church and State:

> Misguided individuals and powerful sectarian lobbies in Washington continue to press for religious majority rule in the nation's public schools. They advocate for school prayer amendments and other measures that would permit government-sponsored worship in the schools. They want their beliefs taught in the public schools and hope to use the public schools as instruments of evangelism. Americans must resist these efforts.

Opponents of religion in the schools argue that the public school classroom must remain secular in order to ensure that all religious traditions are treated equally and that the emphasis remains on academic topics. The places for religious education, they maintain, are at home and at church.

The views of extremists on both sides help to illustrate the perceived stakes on this issue. Conservative Christian activist Jerry Falwell, for example, once expressed hope that one day "the churches will have taken over [public schools]." On the other hand, humanist writer John J. Dunphy describes the public school system as a means of discarding "the rotting corpse of Christianity along with all its adjacent evils and miseries," to be replaced by "the new faith of humanism." Although neither of these positions are compatible with those of most activists, they accurately reflect the fears that activists hold. Those who advocate more religion in schools fear an aggressively secular public school system could drive generations away from their faith. Those who advocate less religion in schools fear a conservative Christian public school system that could marginalize members of other faiths and destroy the American tradition of religious liberty. Because the controversy over religion and education tends to focus on the value of deeply held beliefs and the importance of protecting children from coercion and harm, it is unlikely that it will ever be resolved in a way that satisfies a clear majority of Americans.

1

Religion and Public Education in America: An Early Case Study

Kevin Baker

Kevin Baker is a regular columnist for American Heritage *and has also written for the* Washington Post, *the* New York Times, *the* Chicago Tribune, *and* Harper's *magazine. He is perhaps best known for his four novels* (Sometimes You See It Coming, Dreamland, Paradise Alley, *and* Striver's Row). *Earlier in his career, he worked for the New York City mayor's office and contributed to* The American Century, *a detailed history of the United States spanning the years 1889 to 1989.*

The contemporary debate over religion in public schools is strikingly different from the arguments Americans had over the issue two centuries ago. Until the mid–nineteenth century, public education was deliberately religious and generally focused on Protestant values, often directly criticizing Roman Catholicism. When Roman Catholics living in 1840s New York challenged the Protestant system, they initially faced violence, intimidation, and bureaucratic stonewalling. When a new generation of politicians led by New York's Governor William Seward entered the debate in 1843, they banned all "sectarian" instruction in New York's public schools. This measure did not, however, remove religious instruction from the public school system, as school board members immediately ruled that Bible reading and faculty-led prayer were not "sectarian." It was not until the mid–twentieth century that religious instruction was finally removed from the public school system.

Our interminable national argument about education now seems to have boiled down to the debate over school vouchers, both left and right having more or less accepted the idea that we must have "standards." Moreover, with George W. Bush's recent initiatives to both provide vouchers and aid "faith-based" organizations, the battle has reverted to an even older national argument. When it comes to public schools, just how far should the establishment clause of the Constitution go in separating church and state?

For all the heat generated by this issue, it is doubtful that many on either side know its peculiar and contradictory history—that is, the fact that the American public school system was begun with the express idea of providing religious instruction to all pupils. Or that our nation's fine Catholic parochial school system came about in good part to escape forced school prayer.

The nineteenth-century conflict over religion in the schools came to a head in New York City. Then, as now, it was part of a wider battle over not just what our schools would teach, but what our nation would be. By 1840 New York was one of many states to offer a free primary, or "common," school education, which included a "nondenominational" course of religious instruction. Of course, nondenominational meant something different then: Students would recite a few basic prayers and read passages from the Protestant, King James Bible without commentary or interpretation. This was the result of careful compromise between the myriad Protestant faiths that had long competed for American souls.

A Catholic Response

Amazing as it may seem today, no one filed a class-action suit. But there was still one little problem. Even in the America of 1840, not everyone was a Protestant. In New York City alone, there were some 200,000 Roman Catholics, a third of the city's population, and they had serious objections to Protestant "non-sectarianism."

Catholic parents were advised to keep their children out of the public schools lest their immortal souls be endangered; and many did, while agonizing over having to watch their children grow up in places like the terrible Five Points slums without any formal education.

Nor did it much please the new bishop of New York, John Hughes. Hughes was himself a remarkable immigrant story, a self-made man who had come to the United States from Ireland at the age of 20 in order to live in a country "in which no stigma of inferiority would be impressed on my brow, simply because I professed one creed or another." It was a measure of both his ability and his determination that less than 20 years later he became bishop of New York.

Practical, energetic, intelligent, uncompromising, and sardonically humorous, Hughes would be a ferocious defender of both his flock and his faith. One of the first problems he tackled was what to do about the schools, though here he found himself in a quandary. He would have preferred to build a separate, parochial school system for all of New York's Catholics, but his desperately poor immigrant parishioners were as yet unable to afford such a thing. In the meantime, their tax dollars went to funding public schools that promulgated Protestant teachings, in however mild a form.

Struggling Against Bigotry

Fortunately, the church was not alone in perceiving an injustice here, and Hughes found an unexpected ally up in Albany. William Seward, not yet 40 years old, was a first-term governor who already possessed the independent mettle that would make him one of the nation's greatest statesmen, along with his own vision of a tolerant, democratic America.

In his annual message to the legislature in 1840, Seward proposed, for immigrant children, "the establishment of schools in which they may be instructed by teachers speaking the same language with themselves and professing the same faith."

Seward's speech was a bombshell—and a breathtaking political risk. New York City's Catholics took it as an invitation to petition the Common Council, which administered the common school fund in New York City, for a small share of public monies to support their existing eight schools. Petitions followed from the Scottish Presbyterians and from New York's tiny Jewish community for similar consideration.

The council rejected them all, and Hughes reacted by issuing a magisterial address. "We hold, therefore, the same idea of our rights that you hold of yours. We wish not to diminish yours, but only to secure and enjoy our own." He went on to concede that if the schools could be truly neutral on the issue of religion, the church would have no objection, but since common school history books routinely depicted Catholics as duplicitous and intolerant, such neutrality, he suggested, was "impossible."

In an atmosphere of mounting hysteria, the whole argument reached a grand climax with a three-day debate before packed galleries in New York's City Hall. Bishop Hughes, speaking alone for his church, opened with a three-hour address and finished with an even longer rebuttal. In between, a bevy of Protestant lawyers and clergy lambasted nearly all things Catholic for a day and a half. For all the rhetoric, more heat was shed than light, and the Common Council backed the Public School Society in refusing any funds for Catholic schools.

Decentralization and Secularization

Seward, undeterred even though defecting Protestant voters nearly cost him the next election, made a new proposal, whereby all public education funds would be distributed by the state to individual city wards, which would then decide strictly on their own just what sort of religion would be taught in the local schools.

This early attempt at decentralization came to dominate New York politics over the following months, with at least one public meeting exploding into sectarian violence. Following the city elections of 1842, a Protestant mob attacked Hughes's residence, smashing doors and windows, and was prevented from doing worse only by the hasty intervention of the police, the militia, and a group of Irishwomen who formed a human chain around the Old St. Patrick's Cathedral to keep "sinners off."

By now, new state elections had made the passage of the school bill a certainty. But a key dilemma remained. What would happen to those who found themselves in a ward dominated by a different faith? Didn't they still have some constitutional rights as individuals? The compromise that passed the legislature went a long way toward the basic shape of the public school today. A crucial amendment to the bill mandated that no sectarian religious instruction was to be offered. All public schools would now educate students in the three Rs and leave religion to the churches.

The amended bill was triumphantly signed into law by

Governor Seward, and it pleased no one. Nativists swept the school-board elections in 1843 and soon ruled that reading the Bible in class was not "sectarian." This would largely remain the case for more than a hundred years, until the Supreme Court's 1962 ruling banning organized prayer in the schools. It also served to confirm the contention of John Hughes that a truly neutral public school system was an impossibility. Out of necessity, he permitted Catholic children to attend public schools but refocused all his efforts on building up a parochial system. By 1862, two years before his death, New York Catholic schools had enrolled some 15,000 pupils, and Hughes was known as the father of Catholic education in America.

No doubt modern advocates and opponents of vouchers alike will draw what lessons they like from this nineteenth-century debate. Supporters will heed Hughes's arguments that even supposed nonsectarianism is really sectarian and back the right of parents to give their children whatever education they deem fit, without an added financial burden. Opponents will point to the divisiveness inherent in all attempts to hand over public monies for religious instruction. Indeed, perhaps the most intriguing—and exasperating—thing about the school debate is its ability to entangle political allegiances. Should supporters of school prayer continue to back a common prayer for all in public schools or support vouchers and many different prayers? Will multiculturalists really support funding for schools run by the Nation of Islam—or the Aryan Nation?

Yet there may be a deeper moral here, beneath William Seward's very different, pragmatic approaches, made only two years apart and both to very much the same end. Whether giving public money to Catholic schools or banning religious instruction in public schools altogether, what Seward sought above all was universal education, which he deemed necessary for forging a just and democratic society. Or, as he said regarding immigrant Americans, "I solicit their education less from sympathy, than because the welfare of the state demands it, and cannot dispense with it."

No matter what we decide on the proper boundaries of church and state, it seems difficult to believe that we can today, any more than we could in 1840, dispense with a healthy and accessible public school system and still maintain ourselves as a strong, united nation.

2

Private School Vouchers Are a Threat to Religious Freedom

Americans United for Separation of Church and State

Founded in 1947, Americans United for Separation of Church and State is a political and legal watchdog group that advocates full separation of church and state.

The phrase "school vouchers" refers to policies under which the government provides students with money (vouchers) to attend private schools instead of public ones. Thus the money that would have gone to the public school system is instead given directly to the student to use on a private education. The vouchers movement is driven in part by religious fanatics who would like to destroy the secular public school system and replace it with a religious school system dedicated to propagating specific religious tenets. Students are often not accommodated well in religious private schools, which subject students to religious indoctrination and may freely reject any who do not follow their teachings or attend their religious services. Furthermore, under a voucher system, tuition at these private schools is paid by taxes raised from all citizens regardless of whether or not they support the schools. Therefore, school vouchers amount to taxation without representation. Although a majority of Americans still oppose school vouchers, dedicated politicians and ideologues are capable of putting them into effect—potentially destroy-

Americans United for Separation of Church and State, "Should You Pay Taxes to Support Religious Schools?" www.au.org. Reproduced by permission.

ing the American public school system and doing great harm to the cause of religious liberty.

Legislative measures that would divert millions of dollars from the public treasury into religious schools are being considered in the U.S. Congress. In many state legislatures across the country, bills have been introduced to fund private sectarian education. Some provide for tuition vouchers. Other measures push for tax credits, textbook and transportation subsidies or other forms of assistance.

Ironically, this drive comes at a time when our public schools are more financially hard pressed than ever. Nine out of ten of our nation's children attend public schools, yet some politicians are asking the American people to accept inadequate funding for public schools while they enact new, expensive programs for private religious schools. What's going on?

The Religious Right

A powerful alliance of political and sectarian interests has set its sights on tax subsidies for religious schools. Religious Right activists and lobbyists for the Roman Catholic hierarchy are pressing their demands on both the state and national level.

Religious Right leaders have made their position clear. For example, wealthy TV preacher Pat Robertson regularly attacks America's public education system, calls for tax aid for private religious schools and insists that "the Constitution says nothing about the separation of church and state!"

> *Giving public funds to sectarian schools is the same thing as forcing taxpayers to place their hard-earned money in the collection plate.*

Observed Robertson, "They say vouchers would spell the end of public schools in America. To which we say, so what?" The Christian Coalition, a political group founded by Robertson, aggressively lobbies on behalf of tax aid to religion.

TV preacher Jerry Falwell also bashes public schools. He claims the public school system is "damned" and promotes private Christian schools. "I hope to live to see the day," he once said, "when, as in the early days of our country, there won't be any public schools. The churches will have taken them over again and Christians will be running them. What a happy day that will be!"

The Religious Right has influential allies on this issue. The Roman Catholic bishops have sought government support for their parochial schools for many years. Cardinal Anthony Bevilacqua of Philadelphia once told a Falwell-sponsored magazine, "if we can get [a religious school voucher plan] through in one state then that's the foot in the door. That's what I want. I want to see it passed in one state and let it go through the courts to remove that notion of separation of church and state."

Many short-sighted politicians have responded favorably to this religious school aid crusade. The movement has powerful friends in Congress and many state legislatures. Even the U.S. Supreme Court, once a faithful defender of the "wall of separation between church and state," has let down its guard in several instances.

It's time for Americans who believe in strong public schools and church-state separation to speak out. Consider the following points.

How Religious Schools Operate

Private elementary and secondary schools are usually religious in character. According to the National Center for Education Statistics, eighty-four percent of all private school students attend religiously affiliated schools. Nearly half of private school students attend Roman Catholic schools. Most of the rest attend schools operated by fewer than a dozen other faiths. (In recent years, fundamentalist Christian academies have opened in significant numbers.)

These religious schools do not operate like public schools. They saturate their entire educational program with the sectarian doctrines of the sponsoring religious groups. Children may be refused admission on grounds of religion, gender, academic ability or family income. Church membership and theological viewpoint are important factors in hiring, with administrators and faculty members often selected (or rejected) on the basis of religion. Some religious schools have fired teachers for getting a divorce, for marrying outside the faith or even for expressing opinions on public issues that contradict denominational dogma.

At religious schools, worship services are held frequently, and both believers and non-believers are often required to attend. History, literature and other courses are taught from a sectarian viewpoint. Fundamentalist religious dogma is sometimes offered in science classes instead of accepted scientific concepts. Some schools teach that their faith is the only true one, and other religions are disparaged as "false."

Religious authorities are free to make these decisions without regard to public opinion, and such practices are perfectly legal. Indeed, churches that operate private schools are exercising the constitutional right of religious liberty. These denominations see their schools as a vital part of their teaching ministry, as much a part of their evangelism program as worship services.

Taxation Without Representation

The schools' religious character, however, also demonstrates why Americans should not be required to finance them. Giving public funds to sectarian schools is the same thing as forcing taxpayers to place their hard-earned money in the collection plate.

Americans generously support a wide variety of religious institutions and schools and do so voluntarily. Our houses of worship are among the best attended in the world.

But religious school aid programs would require all Americans to contribute to the churches and other houses of worship that operate private schools, whether they believe in the religion taught there or not. Because taxpayers have no say in the operation of those schools, "taxation without representation" would result.

> *Our legacy of religious liberty is in danger. The nation's vital public school system is being placed in jeopardy at the same time.*

In addition, tax aid for sectarian schools would subsidize the segregation of schoolchildren along religious lines. A diverse society such as ours can hardly afford to do that.

Ninety percent of our nation's schoolchildren depend on the public schools for an education. Only 10 percent of America's students are enrolled in private schools. Scarce public resources should be designated for public purposes, not private ones.

And keep in mind, religious schools are certain to face government controls if they accept public funding. Many religious leaders recognize this fact of political life and have refused to join in the demand for tax support of their schools.

Perhaps most importantly, any form of taxation for religion would violate the principles the United States was founded on. Consider some history.

The Fight for Religious Freedom

America was colonized in part by families seeking religious freedom. These refugees fled the nations of Europe where church and state were united and dissenters faced ostracism, jail or death. Unfortunately, many of these same refugees set up similarly oppressive arrangements on these shores, giving their own religion favored treatment and punishing anyone who disagreed.

From the early days of our nation, misguided religious groups sought to compel all citizens to contribute their tax dollars to sectarian education. Fortunately, courageous leaders in both the religious and political communities stood up and said, "No!"

In 18th-century Virginia, for example, Enlightenment thinkers like James Madison and Thomas Jefferson joined forces with religious dissenters to free fellow citizens from the bondage of state-established religion. Through their efforts, a bill requiring taxpayers to support "teachers of the Christian religion" was defeated. Instead, the Virginia legislature in 1786 passed Jefferson's Bill for Establishing Religious Freedom.

Five years later, following Virginia's example, the first Congress proposed adding to the U.S. Constitution a Bill of Rights. This set of amendments included provisions for religious freedom and church-state separation. The American people through the First Amendment declared that "Congress shall make no law respecting an establishment of religion or prohibiting the free exercise thereof. . . ."

For many years the U.S. Supreme Court barred most forms of tax aid to religious schools. By the late 1980s, however, the high court began allowing some kinds of "indirect" aid. In a troubling decision in 2002 [*Zelman v. Simmons-Harris*], five justices voted to uphold a program in Cleveland, Ohio, that gave tax funding to religious schools through vouchers. As a result, voucher advocates are now pressing for the enactment of similar programs all over the country.

It should be noted, however, that the Supreme Court did not rule that states must adopt voucher programs—only that they may do so under certain conditions. This decision has shifted the voucher battle from the courtrooms to the legislatures and Congress.

The Wall of Separation

As legislators debate the issue, it's important to remember that the American people remain strongly opposed to religious school aid schemes. In 22 referenda since 1967, voters have resoundingly rejected ballot proposals designed to direct tax aid to parochial and other private schools. Referenda in California and Michigan in 2000 rejected vouchers by a two-to-one margin. Exit polls showed that voters from every racial, religious, political and socio-economic group cast ballots against vouchers in both states.

For many Americans, President John F. Kennedy summed up the religious school aid issue well when he said, "I believe in an America where the separation of church and state is absolute . . . where no church or church school is granted any public funds or political preference."

But citizens should not assume that our rights are secure. In light of the Supreme Court's voucher ruling, religious school aid advocates are lobbying Congress and the state legislatures for programs that divert public funds to private religious purposes.

In short, our legacy of religious liberty is in danger. The nation's vital public school system is being placed in jeopardy at the same time. If these vital features of American life are to be preserved, all Americans must come to their defense.

3

Private School Vouchers Promote Civil Rights

Clarence Thomas

Supreme Court justice Clarence Thomas was appointed by President George H.W. Bush in 1991 after serving as a justice on the U.S. Court of Appeals for the District of Columbia and as head of the Equal Employment Opportunity Commission (EEOC). He is currently the youngest member of the Supreme Court, and widely regarded as one of the most conservative.

School "vouchers" are fees paid by the government to send a student to private school. Critics contend that because most private schools are religious, the use of vouchers violates the First Amendment separation of church and state. An Ohio voucher program was challenged in *Zelman v. Simmons* (2002), in which the Supreme Court declared that school vouchers do not necessarily violate the First Amendment. Although the majority opinion in *Zelman* is correct, it does not go far enough in upholding the Fourteenth Amendment's protection of equal opportunity. The Ohio voucher program greatly expands the options available to low-income public school students. Such programs stand to break the cycle of poverty by allowing students to obtain an education and escape from unemployment and low-wage jobs, which may one day lead to progress in ending racial discrimination.

Frederick Douglass once said that "education . . . means emancipation. It means light and liberty. It means the uplifting of the soul of man into the glorious light of truth, the

Clarence Thomas, opinion, *Zelman v. Simmons*, 2002.

light by which men can only be made free." Today many of our inner-city public schools deny emancipation to urban minority students. Despite this Court's observation nearly 50 years ago in *Brown v. Board of Education* [1954], that "it is doubtful that any child may reasonably be expected to succeed in life if he is denied the opportunity of an education," urban children have been forced into a system that continually fails them. These cases present an example of such failures. Besieged by escalating financial problems and declining academic achievement, the Cleveland City School District was in the midst of an academic emergency when Ohio enacted its scholarship program.

The dissents and respondents wish to invoke the Establishment Clause of the First Amendment [which prohibits government from establishing an official religion] as incorporated through the Fourteenth, to constrain a State's neutral efforts to provide greater educational opportunity for underprivileged minority students. Today's decision properly upholds the program as constitutional, and I join it in full.

The Establishment Clause and State Law

This Court has often considered whether efforts to provide children with the best educational resources conflict with constitutional limitations. Attempts to provide aid to religious schools or to allow some degree of religious involvement in public schools have generated significant controversy and litigation as States try to navigate the line between the secular and the religious in education. . . . To determine whether a federal program survives scrutiny under the Establishment Clause, we have considered whether it has a secular purpose and whether it has the primary effect of advancing or inhibiting religion. . . . I agree with the Court that Ohio's program easily passes muster under our stringent test, but, as a matter of first principles, I question whether this test should be applied to the States.

The Establishment Clause of the First Amendment states that "Congress shall make no law respecting an establishment of religion." On its face, this provision places no limit on the States with regard to religion. The Establishment Clause originally protected States, and by extension their citizens, from the imposition of an established religion by the Federal Government. Whether and how this Clause should constrain state action under the Fourteenth Amendment is a more difficult question.

The Fourteenth Amendment fundamentally restructured

the relationship between individuals and the States and ensured that States would not deprive citizens of liberty without
due process of law. It guarantees citizenship to all individuals
born or naturalized in the United States and provides that "no
State shall make or enforce any law which shall abridge the
privileges or immunities of citizens of the United States; nor
shall any State deprive any person of life, liberty, or property,
without due process of law; nor deny to any person within its
jurisdiction the equal protection of the laws." As Justice [John]
Harlan noted, the Fourteenth Amendment "added greatly to
the dignity and glory of American citizenship, and to the security of personal liberty." *Plessy v. Ferguson* (1896) (dissenting
opinion). When rights are incorporated against the States
through the Fourteenth Amendment they should advance, not
constrain, individual liberty.

Consequently, in the context of the Establishment Clause, it
may well be that state action should be evaluated on different
terms than similar action by the Federal Government. "States,
while bound to observe strict neutrality, should be freer to experiment with involvement [in religion]—on a neutral basis—
than the Federal Government." *Walz v. Tax Comm'n of City of
New York* (1970) (Harlan, J., concurring). Thus, while the Federal
Government may "make no law respecting an establishment of
religion," the States may pass laws that include or touch on religious matters so long as these laws do not impede free exercise
rights or any other individual religious liberty interest. By considering the particular religious liberty right alleged to be in-
vaded by a State, federal courts can strike a proper balance between the demands of the Fourteenth Amendment on the one
hand and the federalism prerogatives of States on the other.

Whatever the textual and historical merits of incorporating
the Establishment Clause, I can accept that the Fourteenth
Amendment protects religious liberty rights. But I cannot accept its use to oppose neutral programs of school choice
through the incorporation of the Establishment Clause. There
would be a tragic irony in converting the Fourteenth Amendment's guarantee of individual liberty into a prohibition on the
exercise of educational choice.

School Vouchers and Equal Opportunity

The wisdom of allowing States greater latitude in dealing with
matters of religion and education can be easily appreciated in

this context. Respondents advocate using the Fourteenth Amendment to handcuff the State's ability to experiment with education. But without education one can hardly exercise the civic, political, and personal freedoms conferred by the Fourteenth Amendment. Faced with a severe educational crisis, the State of Ohio enacted wide-ranging educational reform that allows voluntary participation of private and religious schools in educating poor urban children otherwise condemned to failing public schools. The program does not force any individual to submit to religious indoctrination or education. It simply gives parents a greater choice as to where and in what manner to educate their children. This is a choice that those with greater means have routinely exercised.

Cleveland parents now have a variety of educational choices. There are traditional public schools, magnet schools, and privately run community schools, in addition to the scholarship program. Currently, 46 of the 56 private schools participating in the scholarship program are church affiliated (35 are Catholic), and 96 percent of students in the program attend religious school. . . . Thus, were the Court to disallow the inclusion of religious schools, Cleveland children could use their scholarships at only 10 private schools.

In addition to expanding the reach of the scholarship program, the inclusion of religious schools makes sense given Ohio's purpose of increasing educational performance and opportunities. Religious schools, like other private schools, achieve far better educational results than their public counterparts. For example, the students at Cleveland's Catholic schools score significantly higher on Ohio proficiency tests than students at Cleveland public schools. Of Cleveland eighth graders taking the 1999 Ohio proficiency test, 95 percent in Catholic schools passed the reading test, whereas only 57 percent in public schools passed. And 75 percent of Catholic school students passed the math proficiency test, compared to only 22 percent of public school students. . . . But the success of religious and private schools is in the end beside the point, because the State has a constitutional right to experiment with a variety of different programs to promote educational opportunity. That Ohio's program includes successful schools simply indicates that such reform can in fact provide improved education to underprivileged urban children.

Although one of the purposes of public schools was to promote democracy and a more egalitarian culture, failing urban public schools disproportionately affect minority children most in need of educational opportunity. At the time of Reconstruction, blacks considered public education "a matter of personal liberation and a necessary function of a free society" [as stated by James D. Anderson]. . . . Today, however, the promise of public school education has failed poor inner-city blacks. While in theory providing education to everyone, the quality of public schools varies significantly across districts. Just as blacks supported public education during Reconstruction, many blacks and other minorities now support school choice programs because they provide the greatest educational opportunities for their children in struggling communities. Opponents of the program raise formalistic concerns about the Establishment Clause but ignore the core purposes of the Fourteenth Amendment.

While the romanticized ideal of universal public education resonates with the cognoscenti [connoisseurs] who oppose vouchers, poor urban families just want the best education for their children, who will certainly need it to function in our high-tech and advanced society. As Thomas Sowell noted 30 years ago: "Most black people have faced too many grim, concrete problems to be romantics. They want and need certain tangible results, which can be achieved only by developing certain specific abilities.". . . The same is true today. An individual's life prospects increase dramatically with each successfully completed phase of education. For instance, a black high school dropout earns just over $13,500, but with a high school degree the average income is almost $21,000. Blacks with a bachelor's degree have an average annual income of about $37,500, and $75,500 with a professional degree. . . . Staying in school and earning a degree generates real and tangible financial benefits, whereas failure to obtain even a high school degree essentially relegates students to a life of poverty and, all too often, of crime. The failure to provide education to poor urban children perpetuates a vicious cycle of poverty, dependence, criminality, and alienation that continues for the remainder of their lives. If society cannot end racial discrimination, at least it can arm minorities with the education to defend themselves from some of discrimination's effects.

4

The U.S. Government Should Endorse School Prayer

Laurel MacLeod

Laurel MacLeod is an adjunct instructor of government at Patrick Henry College and former director of legislative and public policy for Concerned Women for America, a conservative Christian political organization. She has served as a guest lecturer at Georgetown University and Wellesley College.

Current restrictions on public school prayer are tantamount to a restriction of religious expression. These restrictions come from a series of Supreme Court rulings that have relied on the First Amendment's clause prohibiting the government from making "an establishment of religion." These rulings presuppose that the Constitution does not favor state-sanctioned public prayer, yet the Constitutional Convention itself sanctioned public prayer. The phrase "separation of church and state" appears nowhere in the Constitution; it comes from a letter written by Thomas Jefferson, who authorized school prayer at the University of Virginia. Although many are concerned that some students might be offended by state-sanctioned prayer, these students can be allowed to opt out on the basis of their beliefs—just as conservative Christian students can opt out of sex education classes. Rather than making students more free, restrictions on school prayer make students less free by preventing them from worshipping with their classmates.

Laurel MacLeod, "School Prayer and Religious Liberty: A Constitutional Perspective," www.cwfa.org, September 1, 2000. Copyright © 2000 by Concerned Women for America. Reproduced by permission.

In 1962, the United States Supreme Court ruled that it was unconstitutional for the state of New York to allow the recitation of prayer in its public schools. The prayer that had been read daily said: "Almighty God, we acknowledge our dependence upon Thee, and we beg Thy blessings upon us, our parents, our teachers, and our country."

Since that ruling, many facets of American cultural life have changed dramatically. Concerned Women for America (CWA) recognizes that the issue of school prayer has continued to arise because, in too many instances, religious expression has been denied to students. Prayer does, of necessity, carry religious connotations. The prayer issue has become a fundamental question of whether or not religious expression, in the form of prayer, is appropriate in the setting of a public school.

Legal rulings in the twentieth century have jeopardized free religious expression. As a result, public schools have grown increasingly hostile to the rights of students to express religious opinions. This policy analysis is intended to give clarity to the current discussion of prayer in the public schools, in relation to the Free Exercise Clause of the United States Constitution.

The First Amendment

Twentieth-century court decisions have placed the question of school prayer under the rubric of the First Amendment to the U.S. Constitution. The applicable part of that amendment reads:

> Congress shall make no law respecting an establishment of religion, or prohibiting the free exercise thereof;

In order to answer the question of whether or not prayer as religious expression has any place in public education, we must understand three things:
- The contextual history of the Constitution
- The textual history of the First Amendment
- The origin of the phrase "separation of church and state"

This paper addresses each of these and compares the findings to the decisions of applicable U.S. Supreme Court cases.

Historical Context of the Constitution

When the Constitutional Convention first met in Philadelphia in 1787, the religious landscape of the states was varied. Most states gave official recognition to one established religious denomination. The state of Virginia, for example, recognized the Episcopal Church as representative of the state. Religious belief as an integral part of colonial life was not in question. Rather, religious problems that arose among states centered on the differences among states' established denominations.

The political landscape also bore marks of disunity. The Articles of Confederation had proved insufficient for governing, and the states were fighting over issues of taxation—namely, who should pay the costs incurred by the Revolutionary War. As the Constitutional Convention convened, observers said the idea of a Constitution, much less a nation, was fragile and quickly vanishing. Chaired by George Washington, this meeting of some of the original Founders was seen as a last attempt at unity.

During the Constitutional Convention, states squabbled and self-interest abounded, to the point that no progress was being made. It was then that an aged Ben Franklin stood and said:

> In the beginning of the contest with Britain, when we ware sensible of danger, we had *daily prayers* in this room for Divine protection. *Our prayers*, Sir, were heard, and they were graciously answered. All of us who were engaged in the struggle must have observed frequent instances of a superintending providence in our favor and have we now forgotten this powerful Friend? Or do we imagine we no longer need His assistance?

> I have lived, Sir, a long time, and the longer I live, the more convincing proofs I see of this truth: "that God governs in the affairs of man." And if a sparrow cannot fall to the ground without His notice, is it probable that an empire can rise without His aid?

> I therefore beg leave to move that, *henceforth, prayers imploring the assistance of Heaven and its blessings on our deliberations be held in this assembly every morning before we proceed to business* [emphasis added].

The 81-year-old Benjamin Franklin was not one of the more religiously-minded Founding Fathers—he actually believed more in the rational views of the French Enlightenment—yet he was willing to acknowledge the importance of prayer to the political aspirations of a nation. Not a prayer bound to a denomination, like the states already had, but prayer that acknowledged God as the Creator and Sustainer, prayer that superseded the petty factions of "officially recognized" establishments.

> *The phrase 'separation of church and state' is not mentioned in the U.S. Constitution, because its drafters did not see a dichotomy between their religious beliefs and the document that constructed their Republic.*

After the Constitution was written, the first 10 amendments, known as the Bill of Rights, were added to ensure the maintenance of certain liberties not expressly stated in the Constitution. James Madison wrote the First Amendment "religion clauses," and an earlier draft made his intentions clear:

> The civil rights of none shall be abridged on account of religious belief or worship, nor shall any national religion be established.

When the Antifederalists saw the word "national" in Madison's earlier draft, they argued that his use of that word presupposed a powerful centralized government. That was not Madison's intention, so his wording was changed to the present construction. Yet understanding the wording of Madison's first draft shows that he intended to alleviate the fear that a national church, such as the Anglican Church in Great Britain, would rise to official preeminence.

Separation of Church and State

The phrase "separation of church and state" is not mentioned in the U.S. Constitution, because its drafters did not see a dichotomy between their religious beliefs and the document that constructed their Republic. The phrase "separation of church and state" came primarily from two sources, a letter Thomas Jefferson wrote to a group of ministers and from the U.S. Supreme

Court case, *Everson v. Board of Education.*

The Danbury Letter. Thomas Jefferson wrote the famous phrase "separation of church and state" in a letter to the Committee of the Danbury Baptist Association in Connecticut. He was responding to the letter they had written, part of which said:

> Our Sentiments are uniformly on the side of Religious Liberty—That Religion is at all times and places a Matter between God and individuals—That no man ought to suffer in Name, person or effects on account of his religious Opinions—That the legitimate Power of civil Government extends no further than to punish the man who works ill to his neighbor.

Jefferson's response to their letter was amicable. He said,

> Believing with you that religion is a matter which lies solely between man and his God, that he owes account to none other for his faith or his worship, that *the legislative powers of government reach actions only, and not opinions* [emphasis added], I contemplate with sovereign reverence that act of the whole American people which declared that their legislature should "make no law respecting an establishment of religion, or prohibiting the free exercise thereof," thus building a wall of separation between Church and State. Adhering to this expression of the supreme will of the nation in behalf of the *rights of conscience*, I shall see with sincere satisfaction the progress of those sentiments which tend to restore to man all his natural rights, convinced he has no natural right in opposition to his social duties.

Jefferson's declaration of "a wall of separation between Church and State" expressed his opinion that the federal government did not have the authority to "prescribe even occasional performances of [religious] devotion." He did not question the validity of religious belief, but he constructed his "wall" to protect religious freedom of conscience from the potential of one federally recognized religion. His fears were well founded. In his inaugural Address of the previous year, Jefferson had noted that America had "banished from our land that religious intolerance under which mankind so long bled and suffered." Clearly, Jefferson decried the federal domination of religious freedom through one established church.

In addition, when Jefferson founded the University of Virginia, the Pamphlet of University Regulations included two sections that read:

- No compulsory attendance on prayers or services.
- Each denomination to send a clergyman to conduct daily prayers and Sunday service for two weeks.

Was this a man who would have sanctioned the complete removal of any form of prayer from the public schools of America? Obviously, Thomas Jefferson's views on church and state have been grossly distorted.

Everson v. Board of Education. The second notable mention of the phrase "separation of church and state" came in the 1947 U.S. Supreme Court case, *Everson v. Board of Education.* The plaintiff argued the New Jersey law that reimbursed parents for the cost of bus transportation—to public and religious schools—violated the Establishment Clause of the First Amendment. The Supreme Court said that it did not. In the majority opinion, however, Justice Hugo Black used language to set the stage for damaging rulings in the future. He wrote that the Establishment Clause created a "complete separation between the state and religion." Jefferson's letter was written 10 years after the ratification of the First Amendment, yet Black relied upon his own interpretation of Jefferson's words, rather than on the text of the First Amendment, to set the *Everson* precedent for future rulings.

Twentieth-Century Cases

Twentieth-century courts, based predominately on Jefferson's letter and on the precedent Justice Black created in *Everson*, have argued that the Constitution intended to separate all religious *expression* from public life. Yet that ignores the textual history and the original intent of James Madison, the author of these religion clauses. It also ignores the broad, historical context. The men who hammered out each section of the Constitution also believed in the importance of daily prayer.

The Establishment Clause has often been misinterpreted to mean that any link to religion is "establishing" religion. One of the causes of this is a simple alteration of the wording in the First Amendment. The clause reads, "Congress shall make no law respecting *an* establishment of religion." It does *not* read, "Congress shall make no law respecting *the* establishment of religion," as it is often misquoted. If the article is read as "the," then it refers to establishment of all religion in general. If the article is "an," then it clearly refers to a specific religion or denomination—an interpretation backed up by historical records. Realizing that the amendment uses the word "an" helps clarify the meaning of the Framers. So, rather than attempting to separate themselves from religious belief and expression, the Framers were trying to keep one *denomination* from being favored over another.

> **//** It seems unreasonable that public schools allow open discussion about sex but do not allow open discussion about God. **//**

The twentieth-century cases pertinent to the issue of school prayer do not recognize those differences. They have clearly been built upon the framework created by *Everson*, as summaries of key cases demonstrate:

- *McCollum v. Board of Education* (1948). It is a violation of the Establishment Clause for Jewish, Catholic or Protestant religious leaders to lead optional/voluntary religious instruction in public school buildings.
- *Engel v. Vitale* (1962). The daily recitation of prayer in public schools is unconstitutional.
- *Abington School District v. Schempp* (1963). Daily school-directed reading of the Bible (without comment), and daily recitation of the Lord's Prayer, violates the Establishment Clause when performed in public schools.
- *Lemon v. Kurtzman* (1971). This ruling created the three-part "Lemon test" for determining violations of the Establishment Clause. To avoid a violation, an activity must meet the following criteria: 1) have a secular purpose; 2) not advance or inhibit religion (in principle or primary effect); 3) not foster excessive entanglement between the government and religion.
- *Stone v. Graham* (1980). The Court struck down a state law requiring public schools to post the Ten Commandments (with a notice of "secular application").
- *Wallace v. Jaffree* (1985) A state law requiring a moment of "meditation or voluntary prayer" was struck down as

an establishment of religion because the intent of the legislature was deemed to be religious rather than secular.

- *Lee v. Weismant* (1992). A private, nongovernmental individual (in this case a rabbi) at a public school graduation cannot offer prayer. Student rights were infringed upon, according to the Court, because the important nature of the event in effect compelled them to attend graduation. That, in effect, compelled students to bow their heads and be respectful during the prayer, which the Court ruled was a constitutional violation.
- *Santa Fe Independent School District v. Jane Doe* (2000). The Court struck down a school district's policy that allowed an elected student chaplain to open football games with a public prayer. Even though high school football games are purely voluntary activities, the Court concluded that the policy "establishes an improper majoritarian election on religion, and unquestionably has the purpose and creates the perception of encouraging the delivery of prayer at a series of important school events."

Notice that each of those cases focused on the Establishment Clause to the *detriment* of the Free Exercise Clause. That has been the trend of the twentieth century. The courts have too quickly forgotten that the Constitution explicitly protects the free exercise of religion.

Arguments Against School Prayer

While the Founding Fathers encouraged prayer during the Constitutional Convention and in ordinances governing education, the U.S. Supreme Court has dramatically shifted their original premises. Some legal scholars and special interest groups have built upon those precedents, creating other rationalizations for limiting religious expression in America's public schools.

The most prevalent argument of such individuals is that the government has a responsibility to be neutral, so that no child is offended by the religious speech of another. This is erroneous because the issue *cannot* be neutral. Elimination of religious expression for the atheist will offend the child who believes in God. So, the schools must choose. Since 1962, they have sided with the small, nonreligious minority of atheists which, as a recent *Newsweek* poll shows, consists of only 4 percent of the population. By contrast, 94 percent of respondents to that same survey professed a religious faith, and 61 percent said that they agreed with the statement that "religion is very important" in their lives.

If free religious expression in the form of prayer is prohibited, school officials are, at the very least, teaching children that public acknowledgment of God is not as important as the things the schools *can* discuss. It seems unreasonable that public schools allow open discussion about sex but do not allow open discussion about God. The courts have forgotten that schools can allow free religious expression without *embracing* any particular type of religious thought.

Another argument used against religious expression is that prayer "polarizes citizens around a religious axis." Yet the First Amendment was written to *avoid* the squabbles that might result among denominations. Not allowing prayer has done more to polarize citizens than almost any other issue in American history. Allowing prayer would put decision-making back in the hands of parents and local school boards, where it once rested. Those local boards could set guidelines that would allow students who object to all prayer or some prayers not to participate, just as many religious students have opted out of sex education classes. That would clearly respect the rights of the minority, without infringing upon the rights of the majority. Local school boards would also be protected by the constitutional "time/place/manner" restrictions that apply equally to religious and nonreligious speech. Ultimately, a restoration of free expression to local public schools would unite, not polarize, citizens.

Freedom of Religion: An Inalienable Right

The Constitution grants the free exercise of religion to every American, and that right should not vanish at the doors of a public school. Although the Constitution does not overtly mention God, it does imply dependence upon a Creator through its last words, called the Subscription Clause. It says:

> Done in convention, by the unanimous consent of the states present, the Seventeenth day of September, in the Year of our Lord One Thousand Seven Hundred and Eighty-Seven, and of the independence of the United States of America the twelfth. In witness whereof we have hereunto subscribed our names.

The fact that the Founding Fathers recognized the Constitution as written in the 12th year of independence, shows the Declaration of Independence to be America's founding document. The Declaration clearly acknowledges the Creator God.

The Founders did not codify religion in the Constitution because Congress did not have the authority to govern religious thought. As James Madison so aptly put it, "Religion is the duty man owes to his Creator." The members of Congress did not desire to create a theocratic form of government, because religious belief is not under the jurisdiction of civil government.

Yet just as government does not have the right to impose religion, government also does not have the authority to constrain free religious expression. The Declaration of Independence did not infringe upon the multiplicity of modes of worship in the states, yet it acknowledged God and unchangeable universal principles, as inalienable rights.

That balance is still possible today. Congress must now meet the challenge presented to them. Americans overwhelmingly favor a remedy for the jurisprudence of error that has suppressed their rights of free exercise for too many years. Let us return to our heritage as a free nation, unencumbered by the bonds that have too easily entangled us.

5

The U.S. Government Should Not Endorse School Prayer

Liberty

The Seventh-Day Adventist Church, a Christian denomination that has played an instrumental role in many important First Amendment cases, has published Liberty *magazine since 1906.*

Conservative politicians and Christian groups are attempting to overrule Supreme Court decisions banning government-sponsored school prayer. However, while the Court has forbidden school-imposed prayer, it has never challenged the right of students to pray individually or in groups, even on school property. Students are free to pray provided that the prayer is not disruptive and is not introduced in such a manner as to force all nonparticipating students to become a captive audience, as in the case of formal classroom prayer sessions or intercom prayers. School prayer proponents argue that students who do not wish to participate in such prayers have the opportunity to opt out, but, the peer pressure—and even potential violence—that such students face prevent opting out from being a viable option. Furthermore, the government should never be given the power to set religious norms.

The Bell and McCord children were verbally assaulted at the school, not just by students, but by the faculty as well. Upside-down crosses were taped to their schoolbooks and lockers. The McCords' family pet, a prizewinning goat, had its throat slit. The parents were "publicly vilified" at a school board meeting. Both families received anonymous threatening phone calls at home. Joanne Bell, who went to the school to check on her children, was attacked by a school employee who bashed her head against a car door and threatened to kill her. Later, when she was attending her son's football game, her house burned to the ground. Though police suspected arson, no one was arrested.

These events occurred, not in some distant nation in another era, but in Oklahoma in the 1990s—all because these two families dared to challenge a public school for holding religious meetings during classtime.

The Prayer Amendment

Religious meetings in public school during classtime? In America's exceedingly pluralistic society, it's hard to image a more volatile recipe for religious strife. Yet this recipe is precisely what the House of Representatives cooked up on June 5, 1998, with the so-called Religious Freedom Amendment, proposed by Congressman Ernest Istook of Oklahoma and 150 fellow House members. Though the bill died in the House, the mere fact that it made it out of committee to the floor should warn Americans that their religious freedoms are still under assault, even by those who swear an oath to protect them.

Though brief and wellcrafted, the Istook amendment would have radically altered the nature of religious freedom in America. In its final form, the one defeated, the bill read: "To secure the people's right to acknowledge God according to the dictates of conscience: The people's right to pray and to recognize their religious beliefs, heritage or traditions on public property, including schools, shall not be infringed. The government shall not require any person to join in prayer or other religious activity, proscribe school prayers, discriminate against religion, or deny equal access to a benefit on account of religion."

On March 10, 1998, speaking from the floor of the House of Representatives, Istook stated, "In 1962 the Supreme Court said it did not matter if prayer was voluntary; students could not come together and pray together as they had since the founding of the republic." This amendment would "correct the problems that have been caused by federal courts over the last 30 years and would allow students to pray in schools or even invite a teacher to occasionally offer a prayer."

The 1962 Supreme Court decision referred to was *Engel v. Vitale*, in which the Court ruled that it is not the government's business to compose official prayers for any group of the American people. "When the power, prestige, and financial support of government is placed behind a particular religious belief," wrote Justice Hugo Black for the Court, "the indirect coercive pressures upon religious minorities to conform to the prevailing officially approved religion is plain."

Captive Audiences

What's ironic about the proposed bill is that there was never a need for it. Even without the amendment, students have the opportunity and the right to pray whenever they want, either individually or in groups, at school. They may even discuss their religious views with other students as long as this activity is not disruptive. Students also can read their Bibles, say grace before meals, and pray before tests. Praying may be silent or out loud, as long as it does not disrupt. The limitations apply only to situations in which a student or teacher proselytizes a captive audience or "compels" other students to participate in any kind of religious activity—a limitation that would have been severely curtailed had this dangerous amendment passed.

> **❝** Who gets to choose the prayer? What happens to those students who find the prayers offensive or against their own religious beliefs? What happens to those who do not—for whatever reason—wish to take part in the prayer? **❞**

While the proposed amendment would not have allowed the government or schools to initiate school prayers, it would have allowed students before captive audiences—even over the intercom—to do so. Once that happens, a number of questions arise: What will the content of the prayer be? Who gets to choose the prayer? What happens to those students who find the prayers offensive or against their own religious beliefs? What happens to those who do not—for whatever reason— wish to take part in the prayer? Will a student of a minority religion get equal time to pray to the God of his or her religion?

Will Muslim students be allowed to offer a prayer to Allah over the intercom? Will Jews be forced to attend worships in which Jesus is mentioned? Can Buddhist students offer prayers over the intercom? How about Jehovah's Witnesses, or Christian Scientists, or Mormons?

People forget the power of peer pressure. Students and whole groups would be subject to teasing or alienation for having beliefs different from their classmates. Speaking on behalf of the Religious Action Center of Reform Judaism, Mark J. Pelavin warned that "religious minorities in particular will suffer because it is nearly impossible for a student who wishes not to participate to feel comfortable leaving the classroom without feeling embarrassed or intimidated by his or her classmates, teachers, or school officials."

The bill's guarantee that no person shall be required to "join in school prayer or other religious activity" was no protection either. In numerous rulings the Supreme Court has said that merely pressuring a person, especially a child, to partake of, or even be exposed to, forms of worship that offend them is an establishment of religion. That a Muslim child isn't forced to pray to Jesus or to sing hymns honoring the Trinity, but is merely required—by law—to listen while the rest of the class does, isn't religious freedom.

Nor is excusing the kids from the exercises an answer. As a *New York Times* editorial in 1962 said regarding Engel, the archetypical school prayer case: "The establishment clause is a keystone of American liberty: and if there is one thing that the establishment clause must mean, it is that government may not set up a religious norm from which one has to be excused—as was the case with the children in the New York school who did not wish to recite the prayer," and which also would be the case if the Religious Equality Amendment had been passed.

The End of the Establishment Clause

Besides impacting religious behavior in school, the amendment would have also opened the door for sectarian prayer and the display of religious artifacts in courtrooms and other government buildings. It would permit Alabama judge Roy Moore to continue to display his hand-carved representation of the Ten Commandments and allow him to open each day's court session with a prayer by a Christian minister.

"It is time," Istook stated, "to reaffirm Americans' right to religious expression on public property."

According to Jamin Raskin, constitutional law professor at American University's Washington College of Law, these changes would "completely neutralize the Establishment Clause of the Constitution." The Establishment Clause, embodied by the Constitutional framers in the First Amendment, states, in part, "Congress shall make no law respecting an establishment of religion. . . ." The 200-year tenure of this principle—which has permitted the traditions of religious pluralism and tolerance to flourish in this country sheltering those seeking relief from religious persecution, coercion, and intolerance—would, under the Istook amendment, have effectively been snuffed out.

> *What does it say about the fragility of the Establishment Clause when more than half the members of Congress voted for a bill that would effectively have destroyed the clause?*

The vague language of Istook's amendment left other questions unanswered. Who would lead prayer, and what belief would this person have to have in order to give it? Who draws the line, and where will it be drawn on who gets to decide what religious symbol may be displayed where? This newfound right could also invite religious jealousies and aggressions between groups madly scrambling for the chance to expose their own religious artifacts in government buildings.

Why Not Discriminate?

Included in the mandate of the amendment was that government shall not "deny equal access to a benefit on account of religion." This language has been interpreted by legal experts to mean that private religious schools could not be denied taxpayer funding simply because they are sectarian in nature. Rep. Henry Hyde (R-Ill) chair of the House Judiciary Committee, stated that the purpose of the amendment was "to recognize the fact that where freedom of religion is to exist, religious schools are to be treated the same as secular schools are treated. . . . You can't discriminate against a school because it's religious."

Why not? The whole purpose of keeping tax money out of

the hands of religions was to ensure that people don't work to support religious faiths that they don't agree with. On a more mundane level, Rep. Robert Scott (D-Va.) asked, "What happens when the Catholics must compete with the Baptists for limited school funding? How much better off will churches be once they become dependent on government funding?"

Also, who would have determined how the government funds are divided? Do the Wiccans, Satanists, and right-wing racist separatist religions get a piece of the pie too? What limitations will be placed on these funds?

Government funding for religion and related activities sooner or later entangles church-state relationships and inevitably weakens church autonomy. The inevitable result of this money means restrictions—on how to manage the money, accounting, monitoring, even sanctions when the money is perceived to be used improperly. Soon churches will come to rely on these funds, creating dependence problems. The government admittedly cannot fund all religious groups. Who gets a share, and who is discriminated against?

Fortunately these questions, though still relevant and manifested in a host of other church-state debates, went off the the frontburner along with Istook's amendment. Despite intense lobbying on both sides (the Christian Coalition, strong supporters of the bill since its infancy, expended $500,000 in a last-minute campaign), the numbers 224 for and 203 against narrowly missed the two thirds necessary to carry the House.

The Coming Struggle

The important question needed to be asked here is this: What does it say about the fragility of the Establishment Clause when more than half the members of Congress voted for a bill that would effectively have destroyed the clause? It says a lot.

For now, the Establishment Clause remains intact. But Istook's amendment was just one salvo in the fight that shows no promise of ending soon, Ralph Reed, then executive director of the Christian Coalition, stated, "This we can pledge: We will stay in this battle, and we will keep coming back, not only for this Congress, but in every subsequent Congress until an amendment is passed and sent to the states for ratification. . . . We are confident that we will begin to move the ball forward in this session and that ultimately we will see victory."

Americans who care about protecting their freedoms better

pray he's wrong. Justice Black, speaking for the High Court, wrote that "the First Amendment was written to stand as a guarantee . . . people's religions must not be subjected to the pressures of government for change each time a new political administration is elected to office." Those who won our freedom recognized the occasional tyrannies of governing majorities and amended the Constitution so that religious freedom was withdrawn, as much as possible, from majoritarian despotism.

The prosperity, the vitality, and the growth of faith in America—by far the most religious nation in the industrialized West—didn't happen by chance, but because this country has taken seriously the idea that religion is too sacred, too important, too fundamental to be promulgated and promoted by, of all things, the government. Despite the problems, the flaws, the paradoxes and exceptions, the principle has, indeed, worked well for Americans.

Nevertheless, more than half of the most recent Congress voted for an amendment that, if placed in the U.S. Constitution, would have undone it all. And if that fact doesn't frighten most Americans, it no doubt would have frightened Joanne Bell . . . especially as she stood in the ashes of her home.

6

Public Schools Should Teach More About Religion

Krista Kafer

Krista Kafer is senior education policy analyst at the Heritage Foundation, a conservative public policy think tank. She has also served as an assistant to Republican congressmen David McIntosh and Bob Schaffer.

Because some school officials are ignorant of Supreme Court decisions on First Amendment issues, they do not realize the degree to which U.S. law currently favors teaching religion as part of an unbiased secular curriculum. One Supreme Court case that brought about the end of government-endorsed school prayer, *Abington v. Schempp*, also stated that "it would be impossible to teach meaningfully many subjects in the social sciences or the humanities without some mention of religion." The Constitution clearly permits instruction on a variety of religious issues—including instruction that may involve primary sources, such as the Bible or Koran—provided that teachers do not use the opportunity to proselytize students or criticize their beliefs. As more school officials and parents become better informed on these issues, study of religion in public schools may increase, enriching the secular educational experience.

Earlier this year, a kindergartner named Kayla was told she couldn't pray with her friends during lunch. Her family filed suit against her New York school district, and a federal judge or-

Krista Kafer, "How to Teach Religion in Public Schools," *The World & I*, vol. 17, August 2002, p. 52. Copyright © 2002 by News World Communications, Inc. Reproduced by permission of the author.

dered the school to allow the girl to pray while the trial proceeds.

This situation probably never would have arisen if school officials had been properly cognizant of a string of Supreme Court decisions in recent decades that have clarified students' rights and responsibilities under the law regarding religious exercise and free speech. Ignorance of these decisions has led to school policies, as in Kayla's case, that chill legal religious practice and that cold-shoulder the legitimate and legal teaching about religion in such subjects as social studies, literature, history, and geography.

The State of the Law

According to the Constitution, the American people are guaranteed the right to practice religion free from government intervention. But interpreting the First Amendment clause "Congress shall make no law respecting an establishment of religion, or prohibiting the free exercise thereof" has not been easy, particularly pertaining to public schools. Nonetheless, the High Court has said, generally speaking, that voluntary student expression and the study of religion are protected but proselytizing and school-sanctioned or teacher-led prayers are not.

The justices have recognized students' First Amendment rights to religious expression and to receive instruction about religion and its role in history, philosophy, and the arts. Congress has voted to enforce—and the Court has affirmed—the right of student religious groups to receive the same access and treatment as other groups. These distinctions are well articulated in a 1995 statement of principles by the National Education Association (NEA), the country's largest teachers union, the Christian Coalition, and 22 other educational associations and religious groups.

"Public schools may not inculcate nor inhibit religion," the document says. "They must be places where religion and religious conviction are treated with fairness and respect. Public schools uphold the First Amendment when they protect the religious liberty rights of students of all faiths or none. Schools demonstrate fairness when they ensure that the curriculum includes study about religion, where appropriate, as an important part of a complete education."

While student religious expression and academic instruction about religion are constitutional, school policies vary in the degree to which they are allowed in practice. Some schools provide an open, balanced environment in which students can learn about religions and express their religious beliefs. Other school policies have not been consistent with the law.

Thus, it is essential for educators, administrators, parents, and students to understand their rights and responsibilities under the law and to work together to create a school environment that is both consistent with the Constitution and educationally beneficial for all children.

Teaching About Religion

Religion has played a significant part in history and the arts and continues to do so in the world today. Thus, a wide spectrum of experts contends that religion belongs in a well-rounded curriculum. They say it is essential to understanding the various academic disciplines and developing cross-cultural sensitivity. For example, the late Justice William Brennan, in a concurring opinion in *Abington v. Schempp*, stated that "it would be impossible to teach meaningfully many subjects in the social sciences or the humanities without some mention of religion."

Many educator groups concur. NEA Resolution E-7 says, "The National Education Association believes that educational materials should accurately portray the influence of religion in our nation and throughout the world." The National Council for the Social Studies Curriculum Standards declares: "Knowledge about religions is not only a characteristic of an educated person but is absolutely necessary for understanding and living in a world of diversity. Knowledge of religious differences and the role of religion in the contemporary world can help promote understanding and alleviate prejudice."

> *The same court case that denied state-sponsored school prayer affirmed instruction about religion.*

The Modesto, California, public school district offers a strong example of how schools can teach about religion. When the district launched a ninth-grade comparative religions class, it ensured that the teachers were well prepared. They worked to give teachers a solid understanding of First Amendment issues and content. Teachers attended workshops that included notable scholars. The district understood the importance of the topic and ensured that it would be constitutional and enriching for students.

Many states have established standards recommending the teaching of religion in social studies, the arts, and literature. California, for example, requires teaching about religions in its History–Social Science Framework. Additionally, the California County Superintendents Educational Services Association and the First Amendment Center sponsor a statewide program called the California 3Rs Project, which conducts seminars, forums, and workshops on teaching about religions and student religious liberties. The project supports constitutional and educationally beneficial practices and promotes the "three Rs": rights, responsibilities, and respect in California's diverse school environments. Several other states have initiated 3Rs projects as well.

Religion Teaching's Constitutionality

In California, teachers may teach about the role of religion in history, its artistic influence, significant events, basic tenets, and important figures. The same court case that denied state-sponsored school prayer affirmed instruction about religion. As outlined in Associate Justice Tom Clark's opinion in *Abington v. Schempp*: "It might well be said that one's education is not complete without a study of comparative religion or the history of religion and its relationship to the advancement of civilization. It certainly may be said that the Bible is worthy of study for its literary and historic qualities. Nothing we have said here indicates that such study of the Bible or of religion, when presented objectively as part of a secular program of education, may not be effected consistently with the First Amendment."

Permissible instruction includes such subjects as the history of religion, the role of religion in U.S. or world history, comparative religion, sacred texts, including the Bible as literature, and the study of sacred music and art. The instructional approach must be academic rather than devotional. It should neither denigrate nor promote beliefs or practices. The goal should be to teach knowledge and understanding about religions without favoring any particular faith. Instruction can include a study of central beliefs, symbols, prominent figures, and events. Students should be able to discuss their beliefs in an atmosphere free of denigration. If a student asks a teacher about his or her religious beliefs, it is permissible to give a brief answer; however, such a moment should not be used to proselytize for or against religion.

Teachers may expose students to primary sources. When guest speakers are invited to speak in the classroom, the content of their speeches should be academic rather than promotional. Educators should use care in choosing learning activities. The California 3Rs Project cautions educators not to use methods, such as role-playing, that could risk "blurring the legal distinction between constitutional teaching about religion and school-sponsored practice of religion, which is prohibited by the First Amendment to the U.S. Constitution."

In January [2002], Excelsior School in the Byron Union School District near Oakland, California, drew criticism for its three-week course on Islam. Seventh-graders adopted Muslim names, read verses from the Qur'an, learned to write Islamic proverbs in Arabic, and organized a pretend hajj, or journey to Mecca. The course handout read, "From the beginning, you and your classmates will become Muslims." In response, the California 3Rs project cautioned educators that

> Role-playing religious practices runs the risk of trivializing and caricaturing the religion that is being studied. It's more respectful and educationally sound to view a video of real Muslims practicing their faith than having a group of seventh-graders pretend to be Muslims. . . . Role-playing runs the risk of putting students in the position of participating in activities that may violate their (or their parents') consciences. Such an issue doesn't arise when teachers teach about religion by assigning research, viewing videos, and through class instruction rather than organizing activities that may be easily perceived, rightly or wrongly, as promoting students' participation in a religious practice.

Although the law does not permit the celebration of religious holidays in school, it does permit teaching about religious holidays. Instruction may include the use of religious symbols, sacred music, literature, art, and drama. Such activities must have academic or aesthetic value and be used to promote knowledge and understanding rather than religious conviction. It is appropriate, for example, to hold a concert that includes a variety of secular and sacred music from diverse traditions. Student-created artwork with religious symbols is permissible, but teachers should not encourage or discourage the content of the artwork.

Student Free Exercise

Religious instruction may occur during school hours off campus. Twenty-nine states currently have "released-time" programs that allow students to attend weekly classes on religion. Designed by the local community, programs may include the study and memorization of sacred texts, or discussion of topics like character, peer pressure, or substance abuse. Typically, programs provide an hour a week of instruction for students in grades K–6. Some states have daily high school–level programs.

The Supreme Court's 1952 *Zorach v. Clauson* decision affirmed the constitutionality of released-time religious education. Programs must be voluntary and off-site, and students must have parental permission. Sponsors provide transportation and assume liability for participating students.

Religious speech is protected under the Constitution. Students may express religious beliefs in the classroom and during noninstructional hours, so long as they do not infringe on the rights of other students or disrupt school proceedings. Expression includes speech, artwork, written assignments, and even clothing. Students are permitted to pray individually and in groups. They may read sacred texts and discuss religion with other willing students. Students are allowed to wear clothing with religious messages if apparel with secular messages or symbols meets the dress code. They may distribute religious literature under the same terms that govern the distribution of nonschool-related literature.

> *Schools need not be and, legally speaking, should not be 'religion-free' zones.*

In general, religious student groups have the same liberties as secular student groups. The Equal Access Act of 1984 protects student-led religious groups in public secondary schools that receive federal funds and allow nonacademic groups to meet on school grounds. Under the law, religious student groups must be accorded the same access, resources, or recognition as other student organizations. If a school-spirit club or a chess team meets after school in a classroom, the school must give faith-based clubs the same right to meet. The only difference is that religious groups must be initiated and led solely by students. Teachers may monitor them but may not participate. Teachers may participate in religious activities, such as prayer, alone or with other teachers outside of the presence of students.

Last year [2001], the Supreme Court extended the right of access to private community organizations in *Good News Club v. Milford Central School.* If other community groups such as the Girl Scouts or 4-H Clubs are permitted on campus, religious activity groups must also be allowed to meet. The decision says that speech with an explicit religious message is as constitutionally protected as other speech.

Can Religion Improve Public Schools?

Religious expression is not only constitutional; according to many experts, it is also beneficial. Creating a space for religious expression, they say, can improve the school environment. They say that such policies recognize the value of religious expression, show respect for students' deeply held beliefs, and build trust between parents and schools.

Last November [2001], during the Muslim holy month of Ramadan, New York City Schools Chancellor Harold Levy issued a statement affirming students' rights to religious expression of all faiths and urging schools to show sensitivity to requests for religious accommodation. He stated, "Tolerance for religious devotion is one of the hallmarks of our democracy. I would ask that during these difficult times all staff continue to be vigilant in both respecting religious beliefs and protecting fundamental constitutional principles." Levy's respect for students' religious beliefs and expression provided an example for other educators following the tragic events of September 11, 2001.

Schools need not be and, legally speaking, should not be "religion-free" zones. The Supreme Court has affirmed students' rights to religious expression and the appropriateness of instruction about religion. An understanding of the role of religion in history, art, and current events is necessary for a well-rounded education. Religious expression is protected for students of every faith. They are free to pray and otherwise practice their religion so long as it is not disruptive. Released time provides students with the opportunity for religious instruction off campus. Religious groups by law must be accorded the same treatment as secular groups on campus.

Knowing the law is the first step toward building equitable and constitutional school policies. Resources are available to help educators, parents, students, and communities. The Department of Education, the Freedom Forum First Amendment Center, the Family Research Council, and the NEA, for example, have information on their Web sites.

Opening of dialogue between schools, parents, and community groups can help promote understanding and support for these school policies and programs. In a 1999 letter to educators, then–Secretary of Education Richard Riley advised that "in developing such a policy, school officials can engage parents, teachers, the various faith communities, and the broader community in a positive dialogue to define a common ground that gives all parties the assurance that when questions do arise regarding religious expression the community is well prepared to apply these guidelines to specific cases."

Supported by the law and the community, schools can create numerous opportunities for learning and expression in public schools. Through these opportunities, students will gain a more well-rounded education and a greater appreciation for the diverse religious heritage of other students.

7

Public Schools Should Not Teach More About Religion

American Atheists, Inc.

Founded in 1963 by school prayer opponent Madalyn Murray O'Hair, American Atheists, Inc., is a support and advocacy group for atheists.

Proposed school policies allowing the teaching of religion in public schools are often billed as attempts to broaden education by introducing the teaching of religion into the secular curriculum. They also, however, present opportunities for teachers to impose their beliefs on students by presenting a whitewashed, favorable impression of religious history. Although private religious expression should be permitted by the courts, all religious expression in public school coursework—even if it is part of an otherwise secular curriculum—violates the First Amendment's establishment clause.

A joint document which claims to establish a "middle ground" in the issue of teaching religion in public schools may actually encourage proselytizing of students.

Released earlier this month [November 1999] under the auspices of the First Amendment Center at Vanderbilt University and the National Bible Association in New York, "The Bible & Public Schools" was endorsed by a slew of groups ranging from the American Jewish Committee and the National Education Association to People for the American Way, Christian Legal Society and the National Association of Evangelicals.

American Atheists, "Compromise Guide on Religion in Schools May Fuel Efforts to Proselytize in Classrooms," www.atheists.org, November 22, 1999. Copyright © 1999 by American Atheists, Inc. Reproduced by permission.

"It encourages schools to offer courses in the Bible as literature, explain the role of religion in political and social movements such as abolition, temperance and civil rights, and expose students to the basic ideas of the world's major religions," writes Associated Press reporter Beth Harpaz.

"The guide also steers schools away from more controversial Biblical history," she added, "saying that would require 'a great deal of preparation and sophistication.'"

> **"** *This is an open invitation for religious groups to make the claim that prayer, Bible verse reading and other faith-based activities are all permitted in public schools.* **"**

The document has been under consideration since at least January [1999] when word of the project first leaked to the media. According to the First Amendment Center, the guide promised that it "aids cooperation between schools (and) religious communities."

"These are the articles of peace in our culture," gushed Warren Nord, a University of North Carolina philosophy of religion professor.

Charles Haynes, a scholar at the First Amendment Center, declared that the Bill of Rights "is not intended to make our schools a religion-free zone."

Judy Schaeffer, legal director of People for the American Way, praised the document saying that it would "go a very long way for the well-intentioned."

"But for those school districts bent on using the Bible for Christian faith formation, it won't make a difference," she cautioned.

Studying About Religion

"The Bible & Public Schools" promotes itself as "A Third Model of Fairness and Respect," saying that "public schools (should) neither inculcate nor inhibit religion but become places where religion and religious conviction are treated with fairness and respect." Sections of the guide outline the parameters concerning student religious expression, the right of religious students to organize clubs under the Equal Access Act of 1984, and the distribution of religious literature.

The Guide also declares: "Educators widely agree that study *about* religion, where appropriate, is an important part of a complete education. Part of that study includes learning about the Bible in courses such as literature and history. Knowledge of biblical stories and concepts contributes to our understanding of literature, history, law, art and contemporary society."

After a segue into several legal decisions pertaining to religious expression in the schools, the guide adds that any instruction must be "about religion" and avoid the appearance of sectarian indoctrination. The school's approach when using the Bible is to be "academic" rather than "devotional," and may "educate" but not "promote or denigrate any religion."

"The school may strive for student awareness of religions, but should not press for student acceptance of any religion," adds the guide.

Subsequent sections give brief coverage to topics such as which version of the Bible may be used, or how it can be taught as "literature" and "history."

"An Open Invitation"

Despite the claim that it establishes a "middle ground," though, some separationists are wary. The American Civil Liberties Union says that it has the document "under review."

"This is an open invitation for religious groups to make the claim that prayer, Bible verse reading and other faith-based activities are all permitted in public schools," warned Ellen Johnson, President of American Atheists. "These groups have a poor record of knowing when not to cross the line on violating the rights of others when it comes to religious proselytizing."

"Look, this problem wouldn't exist in the first place if churches and other religious groups took a 'hands off' position on the public schools. They want to exploit every venue, including school classes, to promote religious belief and ritual."

Johnson said that the goal of having "objective" or "balanced" teaching in respect to religion, and specifically the Bible, would be difficult if not impossible in the current social climate.

"Do you really believe that Pat Robertson, or even liberal religious groups, would allow all of the Bible to be taught fairly and openly?" Johnson asked. "There is only so much time in the school day, and students need to prepare for the twenty-first century," she added. "Religion, if it is to be taught at all, belongs in churches and homes."

The Utah Precedent

Another critic of the guide is Chris Allen, Utah State Director of American Atheists. Allen has been involved in numerous First Amendment–related suits, and says that he has seen similar attempts in Utah to "smuggle religion into the public schools under the guise of history."

"We've seen this type of strategy used before," Allen warned. "The Guide discusses teaching about the Bible as history, but doing that in a fair and objective fashion is going to be extremely difficult, if not impossible. A program that promotes positive contributions of religion and ignores or gives short shrift to negative impacts is not neutral."

Allen added that he doubts if even religious leaders could agree on what should be taught in any course which claims to present the Bible as "history," and he warns about content bias.

"Even if you can get agreement on teaching the Bible from a so-called 'academic' rather than devotional perspective, you've got enormous problems about the content. The First Amendment Center Guide says that the Bible has been used in conjunction with social movements like abolition, temperance and civil rights. But are they really going to tell the full story, or just whitewash the role played by religious groups?"

> *They would use selective quotes and sources to portray religion in a positive light and a source of wholesome moral guidance.*

Allen also warned that attempts to teach about religion in public schools often became suborned to the agenda of specific groups.

"In Utah, the Mormon church took over the 'Religion in the Public School Curriculum' debate," he charged. We found that certain "researchers" and "scholars" who were called in to work on the program were biased, or just shills for the LDS religion.

He also objected to the role being played by Charles Haynes of the First Amendment Center, and traced the ideological inspiration for the latest document on "The Bible & Public Schools" back to the Williamsburg Charter movement. "Haynes was representing that group too, and the Charter was signed by a coalition of religious groups and is clearly designed to promote religion generally. Then as now, the perspective of atheists and other non-religious thinkers is excluded or largely ignored."

A Third Model?

Although the Guide underscores the need for token respect of non-religious students, as well as not teaching religion as fact, some groups are already interpreting the document as a green light to carry their message into the public schools.

"This doesn't clarify anything," said Ellen Johnson. "By taking a defensive posture and masquerading under the guise of a 'Third Model of Fairness and Respect', some of the groups signing on to this agenda are encouraging the promotion of religion. The religious organizations will simply ignore or minimize the strictures that do exist on behavior in public schools, and try to exploit the situation."

Both Johnson and Allen challenged the report's claim of "two failed models," one holding that schools should be religion-free zones, the other calling for the establishment of "sacred public schools."

"This talk of a 'third model' is a solution to a problem that isn't there," said Allen. "The courts and the constitution have repeatedly affirmed the right of students to private religious expression, so that's a non-issue. What is at question is whether religion should be an official part of the school curriculum, whether it's prayer at a graduation ceremony or football game, or if it is disguised as a unit in 'Bible history' or 'the Bible as Literature.'"

"Even if you had courses on Biblical history and literature," added Ellen Johnson, "they would probably not have complete and honest content. They would use selective quotes and sources to portray religion in a positive light and a source of wholesome moral guidance, while minimizing or ignoring the harm superstition has caused throughout human history."

8

Creationism Should Be Taught Alongside Evolution

Patrick Glynn

Patrick Glynn is associate director of the George Washington University for Communitarian Policy Studies and the author of God: The Evidence.

When science teachers refuse to teach creationism alongside evolution, they are doing students a disservice. By keeping creationism out of schools, educators have stifled critical thinking. Moreover, although much of creationism has been debunked by science, the idea that evolution is directed by an intelligent being is worth considering.

Critics have decried the Kansas Board of Education's [1999] vote against evolution[1] as a throwback to the 19th century. In truth, though, both sides of the evolution-creationism debate are locked in a 19th-century quarrel, seemingly oblivious to 20th-century scientific developments that have rendered much of their argument obsolete. While the "ol' time religion" and Biblical literalism of Kansas board members have invited great scorn, many of their opponents in the evolution camp share a naively positivistic view of science, nearly as fundamentalist, in its own way, as the beliefs of creationists.

Not that anyone is likely to construe the Kansas board's de-

---

1. In 2001 the Kansas Board of Education voted to restore evolution to the state's science curriculum.

Patrick Glynn, "Monkey on Our Backs," *National Review*, vol. 51, September 13, 1999, p. 42. Copyright © 1999 by National Review, Inc., 215 Lexington Ave., New York, NY 10016. Reproduced by permission.

cision to strike evolution from the state's required curriculum as a public-relations victory for evangelicalism. By allying themselves with so-called "scientific creationists" or "young-earth theorists," the board members did much to discredit more legitimate critiques of Darwin. While one can respect the piety of a person whose literal understanding of the Book of Genesis leads him to claim that the earth is no more than 10,000 years old, that individual should hardly be surprised if the world at large fails to regard his views as scientific. No less an authority than St. Augustine cautioned Christians against quoting the Bible as a science text and warned that by doing so they would tend to render their religion laughable in the eyes of more knowledgeable people. The Kansas board members fell into this trap.

Assumptions Not Conclusions

But if the Kansans allowed religion to encroach all too clumsily on science, they were reacting in part to an evolutionary science that has too often encroached on religion. In 1997, Phillip Johnson, the University of California law professor and outspoken critic of Darwin, drew attention to the then-official definition of "evolution" promulgated by the National Association of Biology Teachers:

> The diversity of life on earth is the outcome of evolution: an unsupervised, impersonal, unpredictable and natural process of temporal descent with genetic modification that is affected by natural selection, chance, historical contingencies and changing environments.

Modern geology has established persuasively that the earth is a good deal older than 10,000 years (the current estimate is 4.5 billion). Most scientists accept that the fossil record shows evidence of macroevolution—i.e., the emergence of new species—and common descent. But the evidence is a long way from supporting the claim that the process was "unsupervised, impersonal" or even based solely on "chance." That is not a conclusion based on data. It is rather the assumption of most biologists going in.

The board of the biology teachers' association reluctantly agreed to drop the words "unsupervised" and "impersonal" from their definition after receiving a letter of protest from the eminent religion scholar Huston Smith and Notre Dame philosopher Alvin Plantinga, who pointed out that while the fossil record may provide evidence for evolution, it fails to establish whether evolution "is or isn't directed by God." But the underlying logic of the teachers' definition—the implication that all life and species can be explained solely by chance mechanisms—remains the official position of the profession, indeed its central tenet.

Lack of Debate

All of which helps to explain why a middle ground in this controversy, while seemingly available in theory, has proved so elusive in practice. The *Washington Post* editorialized evenhandedly enough about the Kansas decision, noting that evolution is a "reality," "no matter how inconvenient," and adding: "This is not to say that there is no significant debate over its mode and character. There is, in fact, a rich and wonderful one." This rich and wonderful debate, however, does not take place, by and large, among biology teachers in K–12 classrooms.

> *Opponents in the evolution camp share a naively positivistic view of science, nearly as fundamentalist . . . as the beliefs of creationists.*

The draft science requirements rejected by the Kansas board had two striking features. First, the draft contained a remarkably heavy dose of evolution, more than most of us middle-aged folks remember from our own school days. Second, it presented evolutionary biology in a manner suggesting an utter absence of controversy within or about the field. The document included a footnote to the effect that students were required to "understand" rather than profess "belief" in evolutionary theory. But the curriculum made no provision for the presentation of dissenting views. The notion that there exists legitimate disagreement, scientific or even philosophical, about evolution was nowhere suggested.

Indeed, experience has shown that it can be risky for a high-school instructor to explore what the *Post* calls this "rich and wonderful" debate. Recently the *Christian Science Monitor* carried a story about a Minnesota biology teacher, Rodney Le-Vake, who raised questions about the validity of natural selection and introduced his class to "intelligent design theory"—the position advocated by some scientists that the order intrinsic in the universe provides empirical evidence of design or creation. For his troubles LeVake was barred by the local school board from teaching biology the next year.

Students are missing out on a major revolution in the sciences, which may . . . hold a solution to the evolution-creationism deadlock.

Interestingly, the rejected Kansas curriculum also featured a component on cosmic evolution, including the big-bang theory. But nowhere did it mention an issue that has generated a vast literature in cosmology—the anthropic principle, or the mystery of the "cosmic coincidences" in the universe, which a number of scientists argue strongly suggest the existence of design. (Unfortunately, the majority of the Kansas board discarded the cosmic-evolution component of the curriculum as well.)

A Disservice to Students

Part of the difficulty here is legal and constitutional. The Supreme Court has ruled against the teaching of creationism in public schools, and any discussion of intelligent design in a public-school classroom might border dangerously on teaching religion. But as a result of these legal restrictions, supposed or real, and the conventional mindset of the biology profession, students are missing out on a major revolution in the sciences, which may, ironically enough, hold a solution to the evolution-creationism deadlock.

The most interesting challenges to the 19th-century Darwinian understanding of evolution have come not from biology, but from new 20th-century disciplines—in particular, astrophysics and information theory. In reconstructing the evolution of the cosmos, astrophysicists have discovered a universe that seems mysteriously and intricately preprogrammed for life. Regardless of how life originated, this preprogramming seems almost incompatible with mere chance.

In addition, information theory, in combination with molecular biology, has revolutionized our idea of life. In particular, it has led to the insight that life is not simply matter, but matter plus information. DNA is in effect a "message" coded in matter. Matter can carry information; it cannot, so far as we know, create information. The question therefore arises, Where does the information come from?

In Darwin's day it was commonly believed that the laws of biology would eventually be reduced to the laws of chemistry, and the laws of chemistry in turn to the laws of physics. But now it has been established that the simplest version of DNA contains more information than is contained in all the laws of chemistry and physics. So such reductionism—a goal at the heart of the Darwinian project—is no longer conceivable.

These are the issues that would light a fire in students and open minds. But thanks to a legacy of bitter legal and constitutional conflict, and to the doctrinal rigidities of the biology profession, students may be exposed to "current events" in every field but the life sciences, as our schools remain locked in a war between two 19th-century fundamentalisms, one religious, the other scientific.

9

Creationism Should Not Be Taught in Public Schools

Thomas A. Demére and Steve Walsh

Thomas A. Demére is curator of paleontology at the San Diego Natural History Museum and an adjunct professor of evolutionary biology at San Diego State University. Steve Walsh is a field monitor and curatorial assistant at the San Diego Natural History Museum.

The primary difference between science and religion is that science must depend on rational evidence and observation of natural events, while religion depends on the belief in forces beyond human understanding and often relies on texts that must be considered infallible. Creationism is argued as if it were a religious doctrine, not a scientific theory—it is based on "infallible" texts and cannot be disproved on its own terms based on any new evidence. Educators are under no obligation to treat religious doctrines as science; to do so would require them to teach astrology as part of astronomy courses and teach witch doctor rituals in medical school. By treating religious doctrines such as creationism as if they were scientific theories, educators would weaken the already lagging science literacy of American students and hamper their ability to understand how science works.

Scientific literacy is in short supply among American students. This problem makes controversial proposals to teach creationism in science classes, along with astronomy, geology, and the theory of evolution, all the more disturbing. The most important questions in this debate are: "What are the differences between science and religion?" "Is creationism science?" and, "Does fairness require that creationism should be taught alongside the theory of evolution?"

Defining Science and Religion

Science and religion are different. Scientific explanations are based on human observations of natural processes; these explanations may be changed or abandoned as additional facts are discovered. Science does not claim that God does not exist. However, whether or not scientists believe in God, by the very definition of science, they cannot offer God's intervention as the explanation for whatever they seek to explain.

Scientists who investigate the past must proceed in the same way that detectives work when solving crimes without witnesses. In such cases, detectives must assume that no supernatural forces were involved. Suppose you are accused of a murder and you have overwhelming evidence to prove that you were 3,000 miles away from the scene of the crime when the murder was committed.

But the prosecutor ignores this rational evidence, and claims that you made yourself invisible, flew at the speed of light to commit the murder 3,000 miles away, and returned an instant later. How could you defend yourself? Could you prove that you did not have these powers? No—it is impossible to prove or disprove something outside the realm of rational investigation.

> *It is impossible to prove or disprove something outside the realm of rational investigation.*

Any judge who heard a prosecutor accuse a defendant of using supernatural powers to commit a crime would immediately rule that the accusation is inadmissible in court. In just the same way, the explanation of material facts by supernatural forces is not admissible in science.

Religious explanations of the universe, in contrast to science, are based upon belief in certain forces that are beyond the realm of human understanding. Many religions also depend on a faith that certain documents are infallible.

Is Creationism Science?

"Creationists" are fundamentalist Christians who believe that the account of creation in the Book of Genesis is literally true. According to creationists, the Earth is only about 6,000 years old, Adam and Eve were the actual ancestors of all living people, and Noah's flood occurred exactly as described in the Bible.

Creationists ignore the basic premises of science. For example, the public school edition of Henry Morris' textbook, *Scientific Creationism*, published by Creation-Life Publishers, states: "It is precisely because Biblical revelation is absolutely authoritative and perspicuous that the scientific facts, rightly interpreted, will give the same testimony as that of Scripture. There is not the slightest possibility that the facts of science can contradict the Bible." This principle directly contradicts the requirement that scientific explanations must be modified when new facts are discovered.

> *Creationism . . . is not even a theory because its proponents have decided in advance that no amount of evidence will change their beliefs.*

Similarly, the textbook *Earth Science for Christian Schools*, published by Bob Jones University Press, states: "For the Christian, earth science is a study of God's creation. As such, it is subject to God's infallible Word, the Bible. The final authority of the Christian is not man's observation but God's revelation." Yet scientific explanations depend on human observation of natural processes, not on supernatural revelation.

These statements are objectionable from the scientific and religious points of view. Who knows who has the correct interpretation of the Bible? Many Christians accept the theory of evolution, but these statements imply that the only true Christians are those who interpret the Bible in exactly the same way as their authors do. They also imply that the fundamental scientific procedure—human observation—is wrong and useless when it contradicts the creationist interpretation of the Bible.

These and many other creationist statements unmask creationism for what it is: not a science, but a narrow-minded religious belief, immune to evidence or potential correction.

Only a Theory

Creationists often insist that since evolution is a "theory," it is only a guess, no better than any other. But in science, a theory is a statement of general principles that explain many facts by means of natural processes. The proposition that the planets revolve around the sun (Copernican theory) explains a great many astronomical facts and also is considered true beyond a reasonable doubt. In the same way, geological examination of rocks demonstrates beyond a reasonable doubt that the earth is extremely old. The theory of evolution explains a tremendous number of biological and paleontological facts, and it, too, is true beyond a reasonable doubt. Nevertheless, all these theories could be altered or replaced if new observations yielded new scientific evidence that contradicted predictions of these theories. Creationism, on the other hand, is not *even* a theory because its proponents have decided in advance that no amount of evidence will change their beliefs.

Does fairness demand that creationism should be taught alongside evolution? Creationists argue that, "You can't prove that evolution is true (you weren't there, it's just a theory) and you can't prove that creationism is false, so it's only fair to teach both." By this argument, astrology, which is based on supernatural forces, should be taught alongside astronomy. And witch doctors, who use supernatural forces to explain disease, should be taught in our medical schools. This is a mistaken notion of fairness.

The fact is, our students are taught science so they can learn to accurately observe facts and to understand how scientific theories are developed. Bringing in religious creeds and supernatural explanations can only impair their ability to understand how science works. Our children deserve to gain scientific literacy so they can solve the scientific and technological challenges of the 21st century.

It's only fair.

10

The Pledge of Allegiance Should Refer to God

Richard John Neuhaus

Richard John Neuhaus has been an active figure in both politics and religion for over forty years. During the 1960s, Neuhaus—then an ordained Lutheran minister—was an active civil rights protester and one of the first to oppose the Vietnam War (as founder of Clergy and Laymen Concerned About Vietnam), and was even arrested for protesting the war at the 1968 Democratic National Convention. During the 1980s he became known as a more conservative figure and as an advocate for the legitimate role of religion in politics. In 1990, he left the Lutheran tradition and became an ordained Roman Catholic priest. He is author of forty-eight books and a regular columnist for First Things: A Monthly Journal of Religion and Public Life.

In 2002 a panel of the Ninth Circuit Court of Appeals ruled that the phrase "under God" recited during the Pledge of Allegiance violates the First Amendment's establishment clause, which prevents the government from setting up an official religion. Although defenders of the "under God" wording describe the usage as rote and ceremonial and therefore no treat to religious liberty, it is neither rote nor ceremonial. Nevertheless, the wording should remain in the pledge as a humble acknowledgment that the United States is not supreme and will be held accountable by a higher authority.

It lasted but a moment, but while it lasted it was political theater to be relished. The wondrously eccentric U.S. Court of Appeals for the Ninth Circuit—more precisely, two members of

Richard John Neuhaus, "Political Blasphemy," *First Things: A Monthly Journal of Religion and Public Life*, October 2002, pp. 91–92. Copyright © 2002 by the Institute on Religion and Public Life. Reproduced by permission.

a three-member panel thereof—discovered that the phrase "under God" in the Pledge of Allegiance is unconstitutional. The judges sided with Michael Newdow, who had complained that his daughter is injured when forced to listen in public school to the assertion that there is a God. One story said that, in fact, the daughter regularly joined in the recitation of the pledge and was embarrassed by her father making a big stink about it. Never mind, the judges know the coercive establishment of religion when they see it.[1]

Well, within hours the entire political order, from left to right and from dogcatcher to President, exploded in outrage at the Ninth Circuit's political blasphemy. In Washington, both houses promptly passed unanimous resolutions condemning the decision, after which our national leaders marched to the capitol steps to sing "God Bless America" and recite the Pledge of Allegiance, with voices raised to full-throated patriotic pitch at the words "under God." It took Jerry Falwell all of thirty minutes after the announcement of the court decision to declare that he was launching a campaign for a million signatures in protest against it. That seemed an exceedingly modest goal. A moral entrepreneur of greater imagination might have set a goal of 100 million signatures, with the assurance that the millions of contributions received would be spent in reaching the 180 million patriotic laggards. Sometimes nothing short of unanimity will do, or at least virtual unanimity, recognizing that the Ninth Circuit, Mr. Newdow, and Paul Kurtz's American Humanist Society are beyond hope.

> *Once our leaders had put on the record their wholehearted devotion to the proposition that ours is a nation under God . . . they felt much better about themselves and went back to business as usual.*

Once our leaders had put on the record their wholehearted devotion to the proposition that ours is a nation under God— a proposition to which, judging by the public evidence, most

1. In 2004 the Supreme Court struck down Newdow's claim on a technicality, essentially overturning the Ninth Circuit's ruling.

of them had never before given a moment's thought—they felt much better about themselves and went back to business as usual, confident that the decision of the Ninth Circuit, which has a commanding lead in the judicial silliness sweepstakes, would, one way or another, be promptly negated. Political theater aside, the Ninth Circuit's provocation obviously struck a central nerve in the body politic, revealing the inchoate but powerful popular conviction that the phrase "under God" says something indispensable about the way Americans want to understand their country.

Above All That

Most Americans, that is. For a different take on the dust-up, representative of a certain sector of elite opinion, one goes—but of course—to the editorial board of the *New York Times*. Eschewing the vulgar atheism of the Newdow-Kurtz eccentrics, the *Times* is offended by the Ninth Circuit's lack of good manners. People of better breeding understand that public expressions such as "under God" are simply not to be taken seriously. They are but scraps of sanctimony tossed out to appease the gullible masses, while their enlightened masters get on with the running of a thoroughly secular society. The editors sniffingly observe that the words were added to the Pledge of Allegiance in 1954, "at the height of anti-Communist fervor." Anything approaching fervor in opposing communism has always been in bad taste at the *Times*. The editors continue, "It was a petty attempt to link patriotism with religious piety, to distinguish us from the godless Soviets." How petty can you get. If you're reading the editorial aloud, remember that "patriotism" is said with a supercilious raising of the eyebrow, and "religious piety" with a slight but sufficiently contemptuous snarl. The editors, or at least some of them, probably know that an officially atheistic totalitarian regime murdered millions of its people because of their religious faith, but that was long ago, and even at the time was no excuse for getting fervent.

"This is a well-meaning ruling," say the editors, "but it lacks common sense." Read: The court has been dangerously imprudent in upsetting the natives. "A generic two-word reference to God tucked inside a rote civic exercise is not a prayer." The grammar gets sticky here, but presumably the editors mean that the God referred to in "under God" is a generic deity. That is not quite the case, of course. Hinduism and Buddhism, for instance, do not propose a God whom one would be under in the way the pledge says we are "under God." Religio-cultural context, plus indisputable legislative intent, indicate that "under God" is meant to refer to the God of biblical religion, meaning Judaism, Christianity, and (although it was probably not in the legislative mind at the time) its latter-day expression in Islam. As interesting is the editorial claim that the phrase is not a prayer. It is, they say, a civic exercise; to which one might respond that any prayer in the public square is a civic exercise, which does not mean it is any less a prayer. But perhaps the key to the editors' meaning is that the Pledge of Allegiance is "rote" exercise. The word "rote" denotes something done routinely, mechanically, or unthinkingly. Maybe that is the way the editors of the *Times* say the Pledge of Allegiance, if they say it. They do not explain why they think less extraordinary Americans say it that way.

Under Judgment

"We wish the words had not been added back in 1954," the editorial continues. "But just the way removing a well-lodged foreign body from an organism may sometimes be more damaging than letting it stay put, removing those words would cause more harm than leaving them in." The phrase "under God" is a foreign body, perhaps like a cancerous tumor, but it is safely contained and does not threaten to metastasize, so let it be. It would be nice to be rid of it, but surgery is dangerous. "The practical impact of the [Ninth Circuit] ruling is inviting a political backlash for a matter that does not rise to a constitutional violation." And even if it does, the editors want to save their powder. "Most important, the ruling trivializes the critical constitutional issue of separation of church and state. There are important battles to be fought over issues of prayer in school and use of government funds to support religious activities." The very next day, of course, the Supreme Court handed down the historic *Zelman* decision, declaring vouchers for religious schools to be constitutional. Now that, in the view of the *Times*, is a battle worth fighting, and the following day's editorial opposing *Zelman* was forceful; one might even say fervent. Fervor in the defense of secularism is no vice; aloofness in the battle for keeping the public square naked is no virtue.

I am glad that the words "under God" were added to the Pledge of Allegiance, and that they will almost certainly stay there. It is true that civic piety, like every other expression of piety, can be rote and empty. It can also be hypocritical. As I have said before, it used to be that hypocrisy was the tribute that vice paid to virtue, whereas now it is the charge that vice hurls at virtue. To say that ours is a nation under God is both a statement of theological fact and of moral aspiration. As a theological fact, it is true of all nations. As a moral aspiration, it is markedly—although perhaps not singularly—true of the United States of America. To say that we are a nation under God means, first of all, that we are under Divine judgment. It is also a prayer that we may be under Providential care. It is not a statement of patriotic pride, although many may think it is, but of patriotic humility. The reaction to the Ninth Circuit's decision was a salutary moment of public witness to the irrepressible popular intuition that, in the words of Lincoln, America is "an almost chosen nation." I do not expect the editors of the *Times* to understand any of this. To those of a certain mindset, the intolerable idea, the truly insufferable motion, is that they are under anything or anyone, even if that anything or anyone is no more than "a generic two-word reference."

11

The Pledge of Allegiance Should Not Refer to God

Elisabeth Sifton

Elisabeth Sifton is senior vice president of Farrar, Straus and Giroux and former editor-in-chief of Viking Press. She is author of The Serenity Prayer: Faith and Politics in Time of Peace and War, *dealing with the history and implications of the Serenity Prayer (which was written by her father, the prominent American theologian Reinhold Niebuhr).*

In 2002 the Ninth Circuit Court of Appeals found that the phrase "under God" recited during the Pledge of Allegiance is a violation of the First Amendment's separation of church and state. Because the "under God" language was added to the pledge specifically to distinguish the United States from the atheistic Soviet Union, it clearly suggests a religious idea. Its supporters know this and are attempting to maintain government endorsement of that idea in violation of the establishment clause.

The loss of precision in spoken or written language is not, I suppose, the worst problem we face, compared with so many other distressing developments in our national life. But the consequences can include real political harm. Take, for example, a pesky case on which the Supreme Court will hear arguments on March 24 [2004]: *Elk Grove Unified School District v. Michael A. Newdow*, which has generated a great deal of linguistic chaos.

Elisabeth Sifton, "The Battle over the Pledge," *The Nation*, vol. 278, April 5, 2004, p. 11. Copyright © 2004 by The Nation Magazine/The Nation Company, Inc. Reproduced by permission.

In the summer of 2002 Michael Newdow, a pro se defendant with several bees in his bonnet about family law, religion and government, won a 2-to-1 victory in the Ninth Circuit Court of Appeals, where Judge Alfred Goodwin agreed with him that schoolroom recitation of the Pledge of Allegiance, with the 1954 addition of "under God" to its text, violates the establishment clause of the First Amendment. The Ninth Circuit then amended this decision; the school district appealed; the circuit court refused to rehear the case in a murky fluster of judicial action that showed its members at loggerheads with one another and with another Pledge ruling in the Eleventh Circuit; and judges delivered papers "concurring partly" and "dissenting partly" with their colleagues. The Rehnquist Supreme Court itself is partly to blame for the muddle, since it's been handing down divided, inconclusive decisions, in this as in other areas, for years.[1]

I'm only an amateur of constitutional history and the Pledge controversy, but you don't have to be an expert to notice how language gets misused in *Newdow*. Lawyers, judges and commentators carry on, as they have for decades, without there being much agreement on the meaning of the words they contest or interpret—"Establishment," say, or "Pledge."

"Prayer."

"God." Or "under." Clouds of sanctimonious verbiage billow in the public space—from ardent atheists like the plaintiff and his supporters, and from hypocritical Christian Republicans who are eager to have this case heard at the highest level.

The History of the Pledge

To cut through the semantic fog, we can start by asking: What is the Pledge of Allegiance and where did it come from? Grammar school is where you're supposed to learn not only how to write and speak (the grammar part) but also the words and texts of our shared civic life. No surprise, then, that it was a schoolteacher, Francis Bellamy, who in 1892 arranged to have children observe the 400th anniversary of Columbus's landing with a little ceremony that centered on a "pledge of allegiance" to the Stars and Stripes that he had written. (It nowhere mentioned God.) Bellamy, chairman of a committee of state superintendents of education, was able to insure that his mini-liturgy

---

1. In 2004 the Supreme Court dismissed Newdow's case on a technicality, in effect leaving the "under God" phrase intact.

of American triumphalism was installed as a regular feature of public-school life.

A Utopian socialist like his cousin the novelist Edward Bellamy, he composed the Pledge, he explained, in "an intensive communing with salient points of our national history, from the Declaration of Independence onwards; with the makings of the Constitution . . . with the meaning of the Civil War; with the aspiration of the people." He had wanted to segue from "one nation indivisible" ("we must specify that it is indivisible, as [Senator Daniel] Webster and [President Abraham] Lincoln used to repeat in their great speeches") to "the historic slogan of the French Revolution which meant so much to Jefferson and his friends, 'Liberty, equality, fraternity'"—but he realized one couldn't celebrate equality in American life: that "would be too fanciful, too many thousands of years off in realization." Regretfully, he omitted the middle term, though he thought the other two were safe and sound: "we as a nation do stand square on the doctrine of liberty and justice for all." (Did he think that justice insured "fraternity"?) Certainly his big-hearted words express a more attractive national ideal than flags have sometimes inspired elsewhere.

> **Fundamentalist Protestants and conservative Catholics oppose Newdow because they want this godly Pledge affirmed as constitutional, but the truth is that they also believe it favors religion—and should.**

Bellamy was well connected, and soon his Pledge of Allegiance was being recited by students all across the country. Over the years, as US soldiers followed the flag into foreign wars in Cuba, the Philippines and France, and as millions of Asians, Slavs, Italians, Greeks and Jews flooded into a once primarily Anglo-Saxon nation, militaristic flag fever grew, along with allegiance to the Pledge. By the mid-1920s, when nativist opposition to new immigrants prevailed in the National Origins Act, shutting the door to many nationalities and imposing strict quotas, a new Federal Flag Code explained how the flag was to be treated and the Pledge of Allegiance to it recited: the rules of a new secular religion.

The Pledge in Court

Bellamy's Pledge offended various groups from the start: Jehovah's Witnesses and Mennonites, among others, objected, as any of us might, to the idolatrous worship of the symbols of state power, and believed, as any religious person might, that saluting the flag contradicted their declared fidelity to God alone, a spiritual commitment that the First Amendment's "free exercise" clause protects.

Yet, as Justice Felix Frankfurter noted—when the Supreme Court ruled in 1940 that requiring students to salute the flag and recite the Pledge was not unconstitutional—dozens of state legislatures thought the flag ceremony was a good way to instill national loyalty in a diverse school population, having them share "a common experience . . . designed to evoke in them appreciation of the nation's hopes and dreams, its sufferings and sacrifices. . . . The ultimate foundation of a free society is the binding tie of cohesive sentiment."

But Justice Frankfurter's 1940 *Gobitis* decision was soon reversed, when Justice Robert Jackson wrote a ferociously eloquent opinion for an 8-to-1 majority that struck down the statutes that, post-*Gobitis*, had enforced salutation of the flag and recitation of the Pledge. This 1943 *Barnette* opinion, with its robust warning against the authoritarian coercion of belief, still holds as constitutional doctrine:

> Compulsory unification of opinion achieves only the unanimity of the graveyard. . . . There is no mysticism in the American concept of the State or of the nature or origin of its authority. We set up government by consent of the governed, and the Bill of Rights denies those in power any legal opportunity to coerce that consent. . . .
>
> If there is any fixed star in our constitutional constellation, it is that no official, high or petty, can prescribe what shall be orthodox in politics, nationalism, religion, or other matters of opinion or force citizens to confess by word or act their faith therein.

Jackson's magnificent, lucid words notwithstanding, Bellamy's Pledge continued to inspire secular sanctimony. And flag worship intensified in 1954, when the [Roman Catholic religious organization] Knights of Columbus persuaded President [Dwight

D.] Eisenhower to add the words "under God." Ike saw no harm in affirming that America, battling against godless Communism, was doing so "under God"—this enhanced his standing with patriotic voters. In an Ike-ish smudge of non-meaning, he added, "Our government makes no sense unless it is founded on a deeply felt religious belief—and I don't care what it is."

President Theodore Roosevelt had detested this kind of mush. When he authorized a new design for a $20 gold coin in 1907, he was relieved that no statute required the words "In God We Trust" to appear on them. To engrave the phrase on specie, this believing Christian said, "not only does no good but does positive harm," weakening the very spiritual commitment it was intended to promote. Congress, however, reflexively favoring banal religiosity, made the motto mandatory on coins, and positive harm ensued.

The Establishment of Religion?

Newdow claims that the "under God" phrase in the 1954 Pledge violates the clause in the First Amendment reading "Congress shall make no law respecting an establishment of religion. . . ." To "establish" a church is to make it a national or state church, but American law scarcely worries about that unlikelihood; rather, the courts repeatedly assess whether the government is favoring religion in publicly funded activities. (The basic worry is about favoring one church over another; secularists worry about favoring religion of any kind.) Does the 1954 Pledge do such a thing? The Elk Grove School District will have to argue that it does not establish religion.

Fundamentalist Protestants and conservative Catholics oppose Newdow because they want this godly Pledge affirmed as constitutional, but the truth is that they also believe it favors religion—and should. They are confident that America functions "under God," that the Founders believed this and that we should say so out loud. Take the Roman Catholic Justice Antonin Scalia. Blithely misinterpreting two centuries of post-Enlightenment political philosophy, he claims "that government—however you want to limit that concept—derives its moral authority from God," that this was "the consensus of Western thought until very recent times. Not just of Christian or religious thought, but of secular thought regarding the powers of the state. That consensus has been upset, I think, by the emergence of democracy." His bizarre argument appeals to "people of faith" not to resign themselves to this deplorable "tendency of democracy to obscure the divine authority behind government" but "to combat it as effectively as possible." Americans have already done this, he claims, "by preserving in our public life many visible reminders that—in the words of a Supreme Court opinion from the 1940s—'we are a religious people, whose institutions presuppose a Supreme Being.'" (It was Justice William Douglas in 1952, but never mind.) Look at "In God We Trust" on our coins and in our courtrooms, he says; "one nation, under God" in our Pledge of Allegiance, "the opening of sessions of our legislatures with a prayer."

> **The voices of millions of believers who dislike noisy declarations of faith in the public square and noisy ministers in the White House have not (yet) been heard.**

True, the Founders believed that all humanity lived "under God," but, as Jackson knew and evidently Douglas did not, as people of faith know and evidently atheists do not, this abstract deism in no way resembles the belief that God created the United States and speaks through its institutions. As good eighteenth-century deists the Founders respected the concept of an Almighty Being under whose aegis and according to whose laws the world turns, but they risked their lives for the principle of government created not by divine powers but by ordinary people using their human intelligence and reason. The US Constitution and Bill of Rights, which never mention God, are the great and crowning glories of the secular Enlightenment.

All too many interpreters since 1954—deaf to these distinctions and trying to be broad-minded—have said, along with Eisenhower, that public mention of God, which is considered anodyne, should be permitted out of fidelity to our national origins. So fine a Justice as William Brennan argued nonsensically that "ceremonial deistic" language is constitutionally permissible because it has become essentially meaningless. These weak proponents of "In God We Trust" rhetoric, unwittingly enslaved to imprecision of meaning, do little to combat the blunt reactionary arguments that distort our Founders' beliefs.

There are other angles to worry about. Thanks to the *Barnette* decision, no child can be compelled to recite the Pledge, but Newdow says that merely hearing the word "God" in it makes an atheist feel excluded from the polity whose citizens "worship God." The Court must decide whether this aural experience is indeed coercive. Newdow's victimization thesis is popular: Think how much of our culture today attributes high moral value to claims of oppression, exclusion, exploitation. Yet contrary to what Newdow says, the Pledge of Allegiance doesn't begin to express the spiritual nature of most Americans' civic life.

The meaning of the word "God" is also up for grabs: Atheists flail about trying to define the abhorrent thing, while Judge Goodwin petulantly imagines it as a singular Judeo-Christian noun offensive to polytheists. His view seems more opinion than fact, as lawyers say, but he has supporters.

Secularists also argue that since prayer is banned in public schools and the Pledge has become a sort of prayer, it should be banned, too. Here again we're in the realm of non-meaning. To pledge is "to recognize the obligation of fidelity" to something, in this case "the Flag of the United States and the Republic for which it stands"—self-evidently a secular act. This is very different from making "an earnest and devout entreaty of a deity," effecting "a spiritual communion with God as in praise, thanksgiving, contrition or confession"—a religious act. The Pledge of Allegiance would be a prayer (or oath, as its atheist opponents and military supporters often describe it) only if the flag itself is worshiped as a symbol of transcendent authority. This may be happening, of course.

The Excluded Center

Meanwhile, millions of Americans who are religious but not fundamentalist (one reliable poll says roughly half of us), including Christians, Jews, Muslims and Buddhists, are just as edgy as atheists are about the God talk, and they deplore what we might call the Scalia-Falwell position. A Baptist minister in the South recently wrote, echoing [President Theodore Roosevelt], "Giving lip service to God does not advance faith, it cheapens it. It takes the language of faith and reduces it to mere political rhetoric. Language that has the power to heal and mend should never be treated so callously." The voices of millions of believers who dislike noisy declarations of faith in the public square and noisy ministers in the White House have not (yet) been heard. The middle ground, where many of us still dwell, as our deist

Founders did, wishing to honor both the life of faith and the idea of a secular government, is treated as if it had disappeared.

Nor has anybody stepped back to ask, Do we really need this Pledge of Allegiance, and if so, why? Frankfurter and Jackson posed and answered this question—in wartime, too—and on March 24 the Justices will take it up again. In my opinion the Pledge deserves to be shorn of its quasi-sacrosanct status as well as of the "under God" phrase, but I may be a minority of one.

Fundamentalist Christians and their friends in Washington are keen to have Newdow heard precisely so they can discredit the secular presumptions they detest and affirm the kind of belief Scalia cherishes. One fears they may want to use the case as a lever to shift the balance; once the Supremes assure them that the Pledge with "under God" in it is constitutional, then local teachers and politicians sympathetic to them might try to amplify it into more openly Christian, even Jesus-specific, formulations. They have a President in the White House who listens to them, a Justice Department sympathetic to their aims, a Solicitor General who is close to some of their principal agents—in short, a perfect political situation in which to further their cause.

For the Bushies and the religious right, Newdow is a perfect opponent, and they're piling on. He's an atheist and proud of it; he didn't marry his daughter's mother and didn't have custodial rights when he started his litigation; moreover, the mother, Sandra Banning, is an evangelical Christian who says her daughter doesn't mind the Pledge. While Newdow's initial case was wending its way through courts in various jurisdictions, he created a legal tangle over parental rights; when the California school district where his daughter is a pupil appealed Judge Goodwin's ruling, it also challenged Newdow's standing to have a say in her education. The Supreme Court ordered briefs and argument on that issue, and asked Solicitor General Theodore Olson to file an amicus brief in the school district's case.

Thus far, Olson has argued that the "under God" phrase in the Pledge is an "official acknowledgment of our nation's religious heritage," analogous to "In God We Trust" on coins and bills. Here we go again: This is the "ceremonial deism" or "historically verified foundationalism" that Scalia approves of for his own dark reasons and that Brennan and Douglas accepted. Olson adds, in a sleazy bow to creationists, that the Pledge phrase can't be any more offensive to some pupils than teaching modern science is to others: "Public schools routinely instruct students about evolution, war and other matters with which some parents may disagree on religious, political or moral grounds."

Thank the lord, though (as we say), Justice Scalia is out of the picture. Speaking at a Religious Freedom Day rally organized by the Knights of Columbus in Fredericksburg, Virginia, a year ago, he derided the Ninth Circuit's *Newdow* decision as an example of constitutional misinterpretation. Justices aren't supposed to comment on cases that might come before them on which they haven't yet heard full briefs and arguments, so Newdow requested that he recuse himself, and Scalia agreed. We know about the cases from which he refuses to recuse himself; perhaps he has calculated that this one is safe without him.

Secular liberals and church-state separationists supporting Newdow gloomily anticipate that, yes, the Court will uphold the school district's appeal. Twenty groups, including People for the American Way, the ACLU, and Americans United for Separation of Church and State, have gamely filed amicus briefs for Newdow and will watch warily as this peculiar father argues his own case, but for them, it's a pain in the neck: They have gay marriages and abortion rights to worry about; even if a godly Pledge is entrenched in our schools as a patriotic litmus test, they think of this as fighting a major battle on a minor front.

The Fundamentalists' Legal Strategy

For the fundamentalists and their friends in Washington, there are no minor fronts in this political war, and an election is looming. Amicus briefs supporting the school district have poured in from dozens of organizations, including the Senate and House of Representatives, and the governors' offices of California and Idaho. Republican politics have swirled around the case from the get-go. (In 2002, Republicans attacked Governor Gray Davis for not being vigilant enough about the Newdow "threat.") And here comes the American Legion, the Knights of Columbus and the Pacific Legal Foundation, a conservative outfit. Then there's the Christian Legal Society, a group of lawyers who want more Jesus in public debate, whose brief has been joined by the Center for Public Justice, a well-known right-wing group, and the Ethics and Religious Liberty Commission of the Southern Baptist Convention, proud of its inside dealings with the Bush White House. "You're not going to run into too many people who are smarter than Karl [Rove]," Richard Land, its president, has said. "Karl understands the importance of this segment of his coalition, and I think the President understands it." Looking out for the mother, Sandra Banning, is Kenneth Starr, Solicitor General Olson's pal and former law partner. Now, how did that come about?

The list goes on: the National Association of Evangelicals, another key group for Bush; Phyllis Schlafly—no party complete without her—of the Eagle Forum Education & Legal Defense Fund; and my favorite, the Rutherford Institute, "a tiny foundation on the far shores of the right wing that advocated a literal interpretation of biblical scripture as a replacement for civil law," as one chronicler described it. We last heard of the Rutherford Institute when it was supplying lawyers for Paula Jones in 1998—lawyers who benefited so nicely from their proximity to friends in Ken Starr's independent counsel office.

Many of these same political activists turned up in November [2003] to celebrate President Bush's signing of the "partial birth" abortion ban. About this happy moment, Jerry Falwell, in a burst of characteristic hogwash, wrote:

> After having a wonderful time of fellowship with President Bush, the president asked if we could all join hands and pray that God will bless our efforts to preserve life in our land. What an astounding moment this was for me personally. Standing there in the Oval Office I felt suddenly humbled to be in the presence of a man—our president—who takes his faith very seriously and who seeks the prayers of his friends as he leads our nation. Following the prayer, I told President Bush the people in the room represent about 200,000 pastors and 80 million believers nationwide, who consider him not only to be our president but also a man of God. He humbly turned to me and replied, "I'll try to live up to it."

The bold calculation of electoral power, the canny conflation of a sectarian agenda with divisive presidential politics, the syrup of piety poured over both—this is Bush's America, a country where fundamentalism thrives in the chaos of non-meaning in secular public space. Richard Land has said, "We're in this for the long haul, and the people on the other side had best understand . . . we're winning." I'm not sure about that, but to prove him wrong we have to be sure we say what we mean, and mean what we say—on the campaign trail, in Congress and in our courts.

12

The French Headscarf Ban Is Oppressive

Maria Margaronis

Maria Margaronis is a London correspondent and contributing editor for the Nation, *a liberal public policy magazine. Her work has also appeared in British newspapers such as the* Guardian *and the* Observer.

In early 2004, the French government voted to ban the *hijab* (women's headscarf) in public schools. Although the law is consistent with France's philosophy of *laicite* (a particularly forceful French policy forbidding any government entanglement with religion), it has baffled many people who see it as an infringement on religious freedom. The Muslim community in France tends to operate on the outskirts of major cities, is underrepresented in the political process, and has even become an explicit target of anti-immigrant politicians such as Jean-Marie Le Pen. Meanwhile, much of Islamic culture in France—especially conservative or radical movements—places incredible pressure on teenage girls to wear the *hijab* for modesty, as a symbol of their faith, and sometimes as a symbol of rebellion against Western oppression. The headscarf ban makes teenage girls within this community targets of state law, placing them squarely in the middle of an overwhelming cultural conflict at a time when they should be left alone by both the government and social movements and encouraged to think for themselves.

For several months now France has been obsessed with an item of women's clothing. The garment in question is . . . the

Maria Margaronis, "Letter from Paris," *The Nation*, vol. 278, March 15, 2004, p. 19.

Islamic *hijab* [headscarf], increasingly in vogue among French Muslim women.

To Americans and Britons used to a more laissez-faire [libertarian] approach to multiculturalism, the French Parliament's recent vote (by 494 to 36) to ban the wearing of "conspicuous" religious symbols in public schools may seem perverse. (The ban will apply to yarmulkes [Jewish skullcaps] and large crucifixes as well as the *hijab*, but no one is taken in by this apparent even-handedness.) Yet similar laws are being discussed in Belgium and the Netherlands; Germany's highest court has ruled that states can ban teachers from wearing the *hijab*; and in Luton, near London, a 15-year-old Muslim girl is hiring lawyers because she can't go to school in her *jilbab*, a long robe she feels expresses her spiritual commitment. Europe's anxieties about immigration and a spreading Islamic revival have found a rich metaphor in this polymorphous piece of cloth, which can be read at once as a cover for inaccessible mysteries, an assertion of Islamic identity or an instrument of women's oppression.

The *Hijab* in French Politics

The French law is meant to protect the republican principle of *laicite*, a strict form of secularism established after bitter struggles at the beginning of the last century to keep the Catholic Church out of politics. Nearly everyone agrees that *laicite* must be preserved—including most of the far right, who take the Catholic *jihadi* Joan of Arc as figurehead for their anti-immigrant campaign. At a moment of perceived crisis, it is a powerful rallying cry. Exactly what the crisis is depends on whom you ask.

France's Muslims, most of them children of its colonial adventures in North Africa, make up about 7 percent of the population; no government has challenged the racism that keeps so many of them in the wind-swept, highrise suburbs (the *banlieues*) on the margins of the cities. A second-generation Algerian is three to four times more likely to be unemployed than a "native" French person; schools in the *banlieues* are bleak and badly funded, experienced by teachers and students as the front line of confrontation. The rise of the far right's Jean-Marie Le Pen is one consequence of this: President Jacques Chirac, who was re-elected in 2002 on the back of Le Pen's success against the Socialists, is mindful both of his debt to his onetime ally and of the threat he represents. (Le Pen is cleverly against the *hijab* ban, on the grounds that it will help the immigrants blend in.)

From the other side, French Muslims are beginning to demand political representation. There are no North African deputies in the French National Assembly and only seven on local and regional councils. A few days after the headscarf vote, a group of Maghrebis [North Africans] from Chirac's own party threatened to quit politics because they are so underrepresented on the lists for . . . regional elections. Meanwhile, as in the rest of Europe, more Muslims are choosing to express their identity through an Islamic consciousness, religious or political or both. Teachers have complained about requests from Muslim girls to be excused from biology, PE [physical education] or co-ed swimming; anger with Israel has morphed into anti-Semitism in the schoolyard and the street. And there's an election coming, with Chirac's close ally Alain Juppe convicted in a corruption scandal and his tough law-and-order interior minister, Nicolas Sarkozy, increasingly setting the agenda.

In spite of all this, I went to Paris unsure what I thought about the *hijab* ban. My instincts were against it, because it infringes personal freedom; it stigmatizes Muslims; it will keep girls who choose the scarf from experimenting and give it the glamour of forbidden fruit; it may push those forced to wear it into religious schools. Besides, it seems absurd to legislate how teenagers should dress. But viewed from Britain, where the government would like more faith-based schools, *laicite* seems worth defending tooth and claw. And, from the outside (maybe the inside, too), the difference between a headscarf worn by choice and one put on because a parent or imam [religious leader] insists isn't always easy to discern.

The Perspectives of French Muslim Women

In Britain, Muslim women say that the *hijab* liberates them (from men's predatory gaze, from sexism, from the pressures of consumer culture); that it keeps them mindful of their spiritual journey; that it expresses an identity they feel is under threat; or simply that it's part of who they are. But at a small demonstration in London against the French law, among the students and solicitors arguing for tolerance and democracy, I also met a veiled child of 9 who said that women wear the *hijab* "so men don't look at us because of our looks, so we don't have people stealing parts of our bodies." The women of the Islamic Forum Europe were kept separate from the men, who told them where to stand and what to chant. Azam Kamguian, who was tortured in Iran and chairs the Committee to Defend Women's Rights in the Middle East, argues that the French ban will give such women a vital *hijab*-free space—that it is the Islamists who suppress freedom of dress, and that veiling children takes away their childhood: "I hate this multiculturalism, this ghettoizing. It's reverse racism in the guise of respect. It's patronizing."

> **❝ *I just wish women didn't have to be a battlefield again.* ❞**

At the Holiday Inn on the Place de la Republique, under the secular gaze of the statue of Marianne, Kamguian's friend Samia Labidi agrees. According to a poll reported in *The Economist*, 49 percent of Muslim women in France favor the ban, as do some prominent feminists and most of the left, apart from the Greens and some Communists. Several Muslim women joined a petition supporting the law in *Elle* magazine; Labidi says women like these are the silent majority, marginalized by media that feed on conflict and ethnic stereotypes. Raised in Tunisia, she wore the *hijab* from the age of 10, when her sister's fundamentalist husband brought religion into the family. She remembers how hard it was to take it off: "The veil completely changes the way you feel. You act differently. It's not a detail."

Labidi believes fervently in a secular, integrated Muslim community as the only barrier against the Islamism she says is spreading like wildfire. She is furious with the government for setting up, last year [2003], the French Council of the Muslim Religion to represent North Africans (and to contain Muslim aspirations): In contravention of *laicite*, the council is a state-funded religious body elected through the mosques. But though she speaks from personal experience and has published a book about her brother's life among the fundamentalists, I can't quite trust the panic in her vision of Islamist revolutionaries fanning out through France. She tells me she doesn't choose to speak in the *banlieues;* when I name the neighborhood I'm going to next she warns me that it's full of Islamist bookshops and purveyors of Mecca Cola, the brand that gives some profits to Palestinian charities.

As it turns out, Belleville feels much like Brooklyn. From a Neapolitan-Tunisian-kosher cafe I watch men in yarmulkes, dreadlocks and Muslim crocheted caps pore over electrical goods that fell off the back of a truck while women, mostly bareheaded, walk by with their groceries. Omeyya Seddik, an activist with the Mouvement de l'Immigration et des Banlieues (part of a broad network of human rights, Muslim and feminist groups opposed to the new law) carefully explains the *hijab* ban in terms of the twin themes of French electoral debate: security (passionate project of the steely Sarkozy) and the notion of a French "identity crisis." He agrees that something has shifted lately among Muslims: "What's new is that there are more public, political expressions with an Islamic basis, and that some women are choosing to wear the *hijab* as a—vague—act of rebellion." But on the scattered attacks on synagogues (which peaked in 2002) he is a little defensive: "It's just violence; it's *Clockwork Orange*." For all his thoughtful honesty I get the sense that he, too, may be glossing over something; that militant fundamentalism in Europe tends to look either huge or insignificant, depending on where you stand.

I ask Nelcya Delanoe, a professor of American history at Nanterre and the daughter of a Moroccan independence activist, what she thinks. She tells me she's seen unofficial mosques multiplying in Paris, in living rooms and basements, attended by men with beards and women in black. Over the past two years women in strict Shiite *hijab* have begun to appear in her classes. As a feminist and a scholar of the Koran, she finds they make her uncomfortable; she invites them to lunch and talks to them about the choice they're making. "In Morocco," she says, "the imams were put in place by [King] Hassan thirty years ago to destroy the left. Now he's gone, the left has been destroyed and there's no one to control the imams. . . . Here too, the left is gone; what we have now is Le Penism without Le Pen. I am against the ban and against the scarf. I just wish women didn't have to be a battlefield again."

"This Thing Has Fallen from the Sky"

Outside the Lycee Suger in the suburb of St. Denis, Samia, Rania and their friend—all 17—clearly don't want to be a battlefield. The say no one is for the law; they don't see why there's such a fuss about a piece of cloth. Rania has worn her scarf to school since she was 14; she accepts that when the law comes in she'll have to take it off. "This thing has fallen from the sky," she says, "because people are worried about Islam." Samia, in pinstriped trousers, corkscrew curls and kohl, butts in: "It's not a Muslim country—it's French—it's Christian." Christian? "Well, a teacher said, 'It's because of you that there's no pork in the canteen'—but there's fish every Friday."

> ❝ *The French law is wrong because it makes schoolgirls the lightning rods for a sense of intolerable tension.* ❞

Samia says she'll put on the *hijab* when she is married; she doesn't wear it now because she doesn't pray that way, and anyway you've got to enjoy your youth. She thinks some girls are forced to wear it by their parents; Rania shakes her head. Rania believes fifteen to twenty girls wear the *hijab* to school; Samia looks incredulous. They're comfortable disagreeing, but when a larger gaggle of bareheaded girls comes up, Rania withdraws a bit. Mirriam is the only one who speaks out for the law, "because we're in a secular country, and we have to respect the country where we are. In Algeria French people can't go around in shorts and sandals. Wearing the veil marks people out as different. At school, we have to be on the same level. And besides, I want to see her lovely hair. . . ." No one wants to argue. They joke instead, about wearing a cross on your front, a Star of David on your back and a veil on your head, about covering up bad hair, about whether I know Eminem.

When the others leave, Rania stays behind to walk me to the Metro. Away from them, she tells me that she wears the *hijab* not for protection against men but out of fear of God: "This life is nothing, nothing. When I go to the next life God will ask me lots of questions, and I will have to answer. When I have to take off my scarf because of the law, God will understand. But the people who made the law, he will punish them terribly." I see that for her the scarf marks and protects a feeling of difference that can't be easily named: She's quieter, more spiritual, less socially at ease; she's private; she's not North African but Indian. What politician has the right to deny her the expression she has chosen for her strengths and vulnerabilities? When she asks me what I will write in my article I tell her I'll say that the law is unjust, that the government has no right to tell people what to wear. But afterward I wish I'd also asked her why she feels her God to be so strict and punishing.

I think the French law is wrong because it makes schoolgirls the lightning rods for a sense of intolerable tension. A crisis about immigration, integration, poverty, political representation and the rise of a fundamentalist Islam (threatening above all to Muslims) is being played out across young women's lives. On one side is the state, with its long history of racism and its alienating language of prohibition. On the other are the imams preaching religion as bulwark and barricade against the West's injustices, hypocrisies and failures. The rhetoric of the war on terror draws the tensions tighter. Banning the *hijab* at school won't rescue girls from fundamentalist fathers or weaken the Islamists, who will exploit it as another instance of anti-Muslim prejudice. Instead, it weakens liberalism. Rather than teaching confidence in rational debate, the law suggests that France's Enlightenment values can't withstand the inroads of a militant religion. And to girls like Rania, who ought to be drawn in and given tools to question everything, it may teach only secrecy and alienation.

13

Fabric of Society: Banning Headscarves Is Right

Gilles Kepel

Gilles Kepel is chair of Arab and Muslim studies at the Institut d'Études Politiques de Paris and has served as visiting professor at New York University and Columbia University. He is author of ten books, including Jihad: The Trail of Political Islam.

The French ban on wearing Muslim headscarves (*hijabs*) in public schools has been roundly condemned by libertarians, well as many radical Muslims, but the motives for the headscarf ban are more political and economic than religious. In the wake of World War II, France encouraged Arab immigration as a means of attracting workers. When the workers became citizens, the population grew. Meanwhile, Arab Muslims living in France have been ostracized from the political and economic mainstream. Too many Muslims in France live in poverty. Radical clerics in the Muslim community have supported the wearing of *hijabs* as a form of rebellion against Western imperialism, which only isolates Muslims further from the wider French community. Although the ban on *hijabs* will not in and of itself solve this problem, it will at least remove one obstacle to integrating Muslims more adequately into the general French population.

Good news. Islamist radicals and U.S. neocons have joined ranks—finally—and buried the hatchet to launch a joint jihad cum crusade aimed at . . . the French. What could possibly forge such a bizarre and unholy coalition of the willing? The *hijab*—the female veil, or head-scarf—worn by some Muslim pupils in French schools.

> *Like America, France is a country of immigrants—except that, until fairly recently, it didn't show.*

Ever since President Jacques Chirac announced his intention to ban the wearing of "all ostensible religious signs" in state schools, firebrand Muslim clerics have taken to Al Jazeera, lambasting the archenemy of Islam, France and its impious *laicite*, or secularism. At the other end of the political spectrum, libertarians and civil-society advocates at home and abroad have mounted a rear-guard offensive (in the guise of a moral crusade) against the authoritarian, racist and freedom-hating French state. Why on earth, they ask, should a few square inches of linen covering the hair of chaste and modest Muslim teenagers threaten France's identity? What's so special about the French—their *laicite*, their cuisine, their haute culture fashion that they so parade down the catwalks of Westernized life? After all, everyone knows Paris has become a mere touristic outpost of EuroDisney. So why the fuss?

The issue is being hotly debated in the National Assembly right now, drawing commentary left, right and center in most languages of the globe. All this is very different from the Frog-bashing and trashing we French grew accustomed to over the past year. Like America, France is a country of immigrants—except that, until fairly recently, it didn't show. Open the Paris phone book to any page, and you'll come upon dozens of names (like mine) that are not French. Poles, Italians, Spaniards, Central European and North African Jews came en masse over the last century, aspiring to become (to quote an old Yiddish saying) "happy as God in France." And many did, judging from the register of France's cultural, political and business elite.

Now comes the more recent immigrant wave—millions of Muslims who began arriving with the end of France's colonial empire. It was a time when France, emerging from World War II, was greedy for cheap labor. At first they were politically and culturally invisible; most were bachelors. But they didn't go back as expected and instead made France their home. They brought their wives, kids and fathered more children in France, most getting French citizenship. Yet the success that previous immigrants enjoyed did not grace them. The '70s and '80s were years of massive unemployment, and unskilled labor from North Africa paid an especially high toll. Fathers on the dole were hardly role models. With no upward mobility, the social attractiveness of French society got blurred. The kids were French; often they spoke no other language. But many felt estranged as traditional engines of integration—the workplace, unions, schools and Army—failed them.

Meanwhile, on the southern and eastern shores of the Mediterranean, Islamist movements started to replace nationalists as the beacons of cultural identity. Around 1989—the year the Berlin wall toppled, on the 200th anniversary of the fall of the Bastille—they made a momentous breakthrough in France itself. Muslim brothers and their ilk started to build, brick by brick, a cultural fortress—those so-called suburbs of Islam. Wearing a veil at school was its symbol. The idea was to erect a cultural barrier, a no trespassing sign. Schooling, the zealots claimed, echoing their counterparts in Egypt or Algeria, led nowhere but to cultural adulteration—a betrayal of Islamic identity that was not even rewarded by jobs.

> *The controversy over veils, yarmulkes, crosses and headscarves is but a symptom. The deeper problem is social—the underlying failure of French (and European) economies and programs to lift up Europe's immigrant poor.*

To them, assimilation into French society amounts to apostasy. By contrast, veiling is the means to rebuild on the shores of impiety a Community of the Faithful. Within its walls the newborn Islamist can find a pious spouse. Children can be raised "traditionally." The great causes of the Muslim world can be espoused as Islamists elsewhere see them: Palestine, Bosnia, jihad in Algeria or the United States. Pressures on "bad Muslims" who do not wear *hijabs*, on Arab-looking youth who do not fast for Ramadan in projects patrolled by *salafi* tough guys, has increased. Videos praising armed war against the infidels in general, and Jews in particular, have sneaked onto Web sites. In class, teaching the *Shoah* meets with hostility, while fights with Jewish kids break out on playgrounds whenever Al Jazeera displays the previous day's scenes of Israeli repression in Gaza or the burial of a "martyr" of the intifada.

These phenomena have been extremely worrying to authorities—and devastating for the traditional French public. Not all *hijab*-covered pupils condone such attitudes, obviously, but the veil is part and parcel of a splintering of the schools and the broader community along religious fault lines. That undermines the very purpose of education: to instill shared knowledge that allows pupils to develop not only themselves, but a shared future and freedom. The controversy over veils, yarmulkes, crosses and headscarves is but a symptom. The deeper problem is social—the underlying failure of French (and European) economies and programs to lift up Europe's immigrant poor.

Critics say that banning headscarves is thus a Band-Aid, a conservative effort to halt the ripping of our schools' fabric. Clearly, it is not meant to cure broader ills. But it stops France's social unraveling on at least one front, and with luck and political leadership could initiate the process by which France finds its way to a new secularist covenant between all children of the country, whatever their origin or creed. Jean Jaures, a father of French socialism, once remarked that the republic could not be secular if it were not social—if it did not meet the material needs of its disparate citizens. In those days, schools spotted promising young immigrants early and boosted them with scholarships into the elite. If we are to ask the new Muslim generation to enter mainstream French culture, we must put Jaures's social elevator into motion once again.

Organizations to Contact

The editors have compiled the following list of organizations concerned with the issues debated in this book. The descriptions are derived from materials provided by the organizations. All have publications or information available for interested readers. The list was compiled on the date of publication of the present volume; names, addresses, phone and fax numbers, and e-mail addresses may change. Be aware that many organizations take several weeks or longer to respond to inquiries, so allow as much time as possible.

American Atheists, Inc.
PO Box 7533, Parsippany, NJ 07054-6733
(908) 276-7300 • fax: (908) 276-7402
e-mail: info@atheists.org • Web site: www.atheists.org

Founded by school prayer opponent Madalyn Murray O'Hair, this organization functions as a support group for atheists and an advocacy group for full separation of church and state. It publishes news, educational resources, and the magazine *American Atheist.*

American Center for Law and Justice (ACLJ)
PO Box 64429, Virginia Beach, VA 23467
(757) 226-2489 • fax: (757) 226-2836
Web site: www.aclj.org

ACLJ was created in 1990 by the Reverend Pat Robertson as a conservative Christian alternative to the ACLU. It supports school prayer and school vouchers and tends to take conservative positions on other issues (such as abortion and gay marriage). The ACLJ publishes regular e-mail newsletter updates and provides resources and legal scholarship on many constitutional issues.

American Civil Liberties Union (ACLU)
125 Broad St., 18th Fl., New York, NY 10004-2400
(212) 549-2500
e-mail: aclu@aclu.org • Web site: www.aclu.org

Founded in 1920, the ACLU is a national organization that works to defend civil liberties and promote separation of church and state. It publishes various materials on the Bill of Rights, including regular in-depth reports, the triannual newsletter *Civil Liberties,* and a set of handbooks on individual rights.

Americans United for Separation of Church and State (AU)
1816 Jefferson Pl. NW, Washington, DC 20036
(202) 466-3234 • fax: (202) 466-2587
e-mail: americansunited@au.org • Web site: www.au.org

Americans United is dedicated to protecting individual religious freedom and maintaining full separation of church and state. Its publications include brochures, pamphlets, and the monthly newsletter *Church and State.*

Baptist Joint Committee on Public Affairs (BJC)
200 Maryland Ave. NE, Washington, DC 20002
(202) 544-4226
Web site: www.bjcpa.org

The Baptist Joint Committee promotes individual religious liberty and full separation of church and state. It publishes the monthly newsletter *Report from the Capital* as well as special reports and action alerts on new church-state controversies.

Chalcedon Foundation
PO Box 158, Vallecito, CA 95251
(209) 736-4365 • fax: (209) 736-0536
Web site: www.chalcedon.edu

The Chalcedon Foundation favors a U.S. government that passes laws in alignment with conservative Christianity. It publishes the bimonthly newsletter *Chalcedon Report.*

Freedom from Religion Foundation (FFRF)
PO Box 750, Madison, WI 53701
(608) 256-8900 • fax: (608) 256-1116
e-mail: ffrf@mailbag.com • Web site: www.ffrf.org

Founded in 1978, the Freedom from Religion Foundation promotes full separation of church and state and equal rights for freethinkers (atheists, agnostics, and others who do not hold conventional religious beliefs). It publishes the magazine *Freethought Today* as well as other material on church-state controversies and other issues affecting nonreligious Americans.

National Center for Science Education (NCSE)
420 Fortieth St., Suite 2, Oakland, CA 94609-2509
(510) 601-7203 • fax: (510) 601-7204
e-mail: ncseoffice@ncseweb.org • Web site: www.natcenscied.org

The NCSE works to promote the teaching of evolutionary theory in public schools and to oppose state laws written to support creationism. It publishes a bimonthly magazine called *NCSE Reports* as well as a significant amount of online resource material.

People for the American Way Foundation (PFAW)
2000 M St. NW, Suite 400, Washington, DC 20036
(202) 467-4999 • (202) 293-2672
e-mail: pfaw@faw.org • Web site: www.pfaw.org

PFAW works to increase tolerance and respect for America's diverse cultures, religions, and values. It distributes educational materials, leaflets, and brochures, including the reports *A Right Wing and a Prayer: The Religious Right in Your Public Schools* and *Attacks on the Freedom to Learn.*

Religion in Public Education Resource Center (RPERC)
5 County Center Dr., Oroville, CA 95965
(916) 538-7847 • fax: (916) 538-7846
e-mail: bbenoit@edison.bcoe.butte.k12.ca.usweb
Web site: www.csuchico.edu/rs/reperc.html

The center argues that religion should be taught in public schools, but in a fair, neutral, and academic way. It publishes the triannual magazine *Religion and Public Education* and resource materials for teachers and administrators.

Religious Freedom Coalition (RFC)
PO Box 77511, Washington, DC 20013
(540) 370-4200
e-mail: support@rfcnet.org • Web site: www.rfcnet.org

The RFC promotes religious freedom but also supports laws that affirm conservative Christian principles and opposes strict separation of church and state. It publishes the newsletter *Religious Freedom Quarterly* and provides regular reports on political controversies.

Rockford Institute Center on Religion and Society
934 N. Main St., Rockford, IL 61103
(815) 964-5053 • fax: (815) 965-1826
e-mail: rkfdinst@bossnt.com

The center is a research and educational organization that advocates a more public role for religion and religious values in American life. It publishes the quarterly *This World: A Journal of Religion and Public Life* and the monthly *Religion and Society Report*.

Bibliography

Books

Robert S. Alley — *Without a Prayer: Religious Expression in Public Schools.* Amherst, NY: Prometheus, 1996.

Clint Bolick — *Voucher Wars: Waging the Legal Battle over School Choice.* Washington, DC: Cato Institute, 2003.

Melissa M. Deckman — *School Board Battles: The Christian Right in Local Politics.* Washington, DC: Georgetown University Press, 2004.

Joan DelFattore — *The Fourth R: Conflicts over Religion in America's Public Schools.* New Haven, CT: Yale University Press, 2004.

William Dembski and Michael Ruse, eds. — *Debating Design: From Darwin to DNA.* Cambridge: Cambridge University Press, 2004.

R. Kenneth Godwin and Frank R. Kemerer — *School Choice Tradeoffs: Liberty, Equity, and Diversity.* Austin: University of Texas Press, 2002.

Daniel McGroarty — *Trinnietta Gets a Chance: Six Families and Their School Choice Experience.* Washington, DC: Heritage, 2004.

National Academy of Sciences — *Science and Creationism.* Washington, DC: National Academy Press, 1999.

Frank S. Ravitch — *School Prayer and Discrimination: The Civil Rights of Religious Minorities and Dissenters.* Boston: Northeastern University Press, 2001.

James T. Sears and James C. Carper — *Curriculum, Religion, and Public Education: Conversations for an Enlarging Public Square.* New York: Teachers College, 1998.

Periodicals

Black Issues in Higher Education — "Study: Voucher Students Perform Same as Public School Peers," January 15, 2004.

Rob Boston — "Devious Design," *Church and State*, November 2003.

Glenn Branch — "Creationists and the Grand Canyon," *Humanist*, March/April 2004.

Pamela Colloff — "They Haven't Got a Prayer," *Texas Monthly*, November 2000.

Jennifer K. Covino — "Choice Is Good," *District Administration*, November 2003.

Kenneth C. Davis — "Jefferson, Madison, Newdow?" *New York Times*, March 26, 2004.

Keith Devlin — "Snake Eyes in the Garden of Eden," *Sciences*, July 2000.

Ed Doerr — "Teaching About Religion," *Humanist*, November 1998.

Thomas J. Geelan — "When Creationism Goes to School," *Free Inquiry*, Spring 2000.

Marie Gryphon and Emily A. Meyer — "Will Schools Ever Be Free from the Chains of State Control?" *USA Today*, March 2004.

L. Kirk Hagen — "Creationism's Expanding Universe," *Skeptic*, Fall 2003.

Samah Jabr — "Hijab in the West," *Washington Report on Middle East Affairs*, April 2004.

Nicholas P. Miller — "Life, the Universe, and Everything Constitutional: Origins in the Public Schools," *Journal of Church and State*, Summer 2001.

Barbara Miner — "Not the Ticket: Why Vouchers Undermine Public Education," *Mothering*, November/December 2003.

Elizabeth Nickson — "The Odds Are on God," *Spectator*, May 12, 2001.

Warren A. Nord — "The Relevance of Religion to the Curriculum," *School Administrator*, January 1999.

David G. Savage — "Justices Keep 'God' in Pledge of Allegiance," *Los Angeles Times*, June 15, 2004.

Stuart Taylor Jr. — "Prayer and Creationism: Met with Supreme Hostility," *National Journal*, July 15, 2000.

Matthew Yglesias — "The Verdict on Vouchers," *American Prospect*, February 2004.

Internet Sources

William A. Dembski — "Five Questions a Darwinist Would Rather Dodge," *Citizen,* www.family.org/cforum/citizenmag/webonly/a0031659.cfm.

Annie Laurie Gaylor — "The Case Against School Prayer," Freedom from Religion Foundation, www.ffrf.org/issues/?t=schoolprayer.txt.

Index